HEAVENLY MESSAGE

My Journey To Natalie's Song

HELEN NICOL

love, always

Helen

Stellium Books
Grant Park IL 60940 USA
Baytype Digital Print UK

Cover Art by Annette Munnich
First Edition Published 2018 By Stellium Books, Grant Park Il 60940
and Heavenly Message Publishing

ISBN 978-1916443938
Baytype Digital Print UK
www.baytype-digital-print.co.uk

This is a true story based on the author's own views and experience of life and matters regarding death, the afterlife and reincarnation. The information imparted is the author's own interpretation of her knowledge, experience and contact with the spirit world.

All physical and mental illnesses should be assessed by appropriate Health Care Professionals before Alternative Therapy is sought, advised or given. Neither author nor publisher can be held liable for any upset, illness, loss or damage whatsoever, which may arise from use of this book or any information therein.

All parties therein named or not where possible, have been given the opportunity to read and accept all the author's views and records of events prior to its publication. All named parties have given permission for their name and stories to be included.

To my mum for her never-ending love and guidance.

To my family and friends for their patience and support.

AUTHOR'S NOTE

Many of us walk through life while experiencing challenges of varying degrees. How we perceive them may have a great impact on how we overcome them. Many of these difficulties are non-physical so may remain unnoticed and untreated. The journey of grief can be an unavoidable individualistic, solitary and destructive road to travel, but it can also be an enlightening experience, making us stronger than before.

I was privileged to have my wonderful daughter in my life and am even more fortunate to have her walk with me through my Earth journey. Her courage and determination in life and in the spirit world inspires me to be like her. Without her help and intervention from spirit guides, I question whether I would still be here today.

Helen Nicol

"The day science begins to study non-physical phenomena, it will make more progress in one decade than in all the previous centuries of its existence.To understand the true nature of the universe, one must think it terms of energy, frequency and vibration."

Nikola Tesla

CONTENTS

THE BEGINNING OF THE END

Saying Goodbye

I had been expecting this day for weeks, but the reality of it all would probably take a lifetime to register in my brain. I am not sure what weighed heavier while I trudged to the corner shop – my heart or my legs. I was like a child who should have an adult accompanying it with the errand. The goal of fetching provisions from the local shop had been achieved, but where I was to go thereafter dumbfounded me. I shuffled down many walk-ways, only to end up back where I started. Silent tears rolled down my face as the feeling of helplessness folded over me. In desperation, I heard my voice cry out: "Help me, I shouldn't be doing this!" My words bounced back at me as the sky burl above and the ground crept closer. Everything seemed transparent and had lost all sense of energy and colour. I became alienated; nothing made sense. It felt as if someone had slapped my face with such force that my soul was catapulted out of my body, flying high, searching for what I had just lost. My cries for help must have been heard as I found myself walking down a street which led to my house. I prepared lunch for my family, then fell into bed. My eyes closed as the traumatic events of the last few hours rolled through my mind.

We had no idea how long Natalie had left in this world, so my family members and I all lived under one roof to care for her and to hold on to every last moment with her. She was on a morphine infusion pump and had been nil by mouth for some time. Now and then she seemed to be present in her body when she gave fight, trying to cough before falling into another deep sleep. Each time she surfaced, the further away she appeared. I religiously held her hand, hoping she could sense that I was with her.

Eventually, she appeared on the brink of letting go, so her family gathered around at eleven o'clock in the morning. A few hours earlier, a beautiful Princess had been born to Prince William and the Duchess of Cambridge. My heart sank – a beautiful princess had come into this world and our beautiful Princess had to leave. The doctor broke the news six weeks previously that Natalie had weeks to months left to live. Natalie's reply to the devastating news was: 'Keep it Happy.' Her family tried to keep it upbeat throughout the process. We played music constantly as she loved music, especially songs by Example and her hero Calvin Harris. 'Cheerleader' by

Felix Jaehn sounded out on the television music channel. It accompanied Natalie on her last journey so it will be stuck in my brain for evermore.

I was trying hard to be happy and brave like her, but the anguish was too overwhelming. As the end neared, she put up a great fight to stay in this world and it was hard to watch. I phoned the on-call doctor to help her; I could watch her struggle no more. Some of the family thought I was being over-dramatic, but I could sense what she was going through; it was time. A doctor unknown to us arrived and gave us all a sympathetic nod and without a word, gave Natalie a final injection of morphine. He tried to reassure us by saying: "It will not be long now." Gracefully, he left when he could see she had settled down again, leaving us all praying for her struggle to end.

When Natalie was aware she was going to die, I tried my best to console her and coach her through what to expect when she passed over to the other world. We hugged as we talked about how she would be given a homecoming party - oh, how she loved parties. I tried to help her with the thought of her last moments by telling her that when the time came, she was to fly as high and as quickly as she could and not look back. I told her that I would be crying, but she was to understand this was just something I had to do. I did not want her to struggle any more, so while my heart was breaking at the thought of losing her, for her sake I knew it was time to let her go. My mind was trying to tell her to *fly, baby, fly*. I was aware that some people in the room did not share the same belief as Natalie and I did, but I could not keep my thoughts silent any longer. I needed to know she could hear me so called out: "Fly, baby, fly. Go to Nana!" over and over. I prayed with the rest of the family: "Please, take her!" we cried.

I held my daughter's hand, while tears were streaming down my face. Unknown to anyone else, I was concentrating on giving her the last healing session that she would ever have in this world. I wanted to do this, because I was aware that it can sometimes give people a boost to help them pass over to the other side. Maybe this is why I felt what I did when she was ready to let go. Due to this experience, I know in my heart she lives on in another way. I felt what I can only describe or explain as her soul energy racing to the top of her body and a folding-over sensation like a ripple towards her feet. Then there was a brisk firm tugging sensation followed by a flowing current away from her at a forty-five-degree angle. As the current dispersed, the true essence of her was gone. I hoped she was flying high as fast as she could and not looking back. Her mouth opened as if to try and take in air but it only opened and shut; her pulsating heart gave one last shuddering beat until all movement in her ceased. There was great relief in the room. "She did it! She did it!" we cried.

An uncontrollable wail escaped from my mouth as my concentration of helping her switched suddenly to the unbearable pain of losing her. I felt guilty for expressing such a big display of grief, because I was not in my own home and there were eight other family members in the room who were also suffering. My hand was fused to hers; when the time came to let go, I couldn't. I cried: "I can't let go, I can't let go of her hand!" My eldest son stepped forward to give me a supportive hug and help me to let go. Collectively we, her family, called her time of death eleven fifteen on the morning of 2nd May 2015. This was the day I knew my life would never be the same.

My Path to Destruction

My daughter was gone. Where she had gone to caused me great confusion and sorrow. The bigger question of why she was gone will more than likely never be answered. Part of me left that day and was flying high with her. I am unsure if that part of me will ever come back. I fully understand people who want to leave this world, people who feel life is too much to bear and successfully take their own life. Having a focus helps. Up until that point my energy had been used to help and coach my daughter on how to die. I was lost in a new world of an unknown purpose. My focus needed to be changed – to what, I did not know. I thought: *what will I do now, how will I ever fill the huge void that fills every inch of me? What is the point of going on, what has my life been about and what in life will make me want to stay?*

I did not want to think about anything or do anything, but the responsibility of giving my daughter a good send-off was my immediate focus. The funeral arrangements had been pre-arranged, but the funeral flowers were to be done by my mum with my help. My mum has a flair for flower-arranging. I hope that one day in the future we will enjoy doing flower arrangements for my boys' weddings, but organising my daughter's wedding was an event my mum and I had discussed and looked forward to. Little did we know it would be funeral flowers we would be arranging for her. My mum was completely focused in giving her a purple butterfly tribute flower and a huge casket spray – a beautiful flower arrangement for over her coffin. I have no idea how my mum was able to compose herself and produce such a wonderful display for our girl.

It felt as if I was still holding Natalie's hand while accompanying her to her resting place and could almost feel the love emanating from the flowers for her. As I walked into the church, the sun suddenly shone brightly onto me and onto Natalie's coffin and remained illuminating the congregation until after the service. Natalie was well-liked by many people, so the minister had a job of squashing everyone into the church to hear a most fitting eulogy of Natalie's short but colourful life. A story, highlighting her life and death and of the traffic jam which occurred after the service due to it being so well-attended reached the Stirling Observer and the Daily Record newspapers the following week.

I was able to bear the sight of Natalie's coffin at the funeral, because Natalie made contact with me through a gifted medium called Patsy three days after she died. Natalie said: "Hi mum, I'm fine, I made it here okay." These are words Natalie always used when she phoned me in life to let me know she had got to where she was going. She told me she enjoyed the homecoming party and continued to say: "It's like there's a hole in the sky. I can see you all; I can see everything but can't get to you." She advised me to go and see 'the body', because she thought it would help me. I asked the funeral staff to open up the viewing room late at night, hours before the funeral, so I could be with her one last time. This indeed made the sight of the coffin and saying 'goodbye' more bearable on the day.

Natalie described in detail what had happened in the room during the few days and moments up until she arrived on the other side. She stressed how much she fought her death, because she did not want to leave me. Patsy had to pause for a while during the reading as Natalie was making others who were with her laugh. She was telling them I was hiding in my son's outdoor playhouse away from the rest of my family so I could continue with the phone reading without their knowledge. My family did not have the same belief about the afterlife so I wanted the reading in private. Natalie said she did not care who was there, what was said or what had happened. She just wanted me to hold her hand through it all.

Natalie validated the reading by talking about many things only she and I would know. I have no doubt it was her making contact, especially when she said 'goodbye' as she ended the contact with: "I'm sending you love with rose petals."

Natalie had a much-wanted white hamster called Domino when she was young. While he was ill, I taught her how to give healing therapy to the hamster. I showed her how to send love at the end of a healing session. My own personal way of doing this is to visualise sending out pink or red rose petals. Only Natalie knew this. I was overcome by the sight of her coffin disappearing behind a weighted curtain, but my contact with her gave me reassurance and the strength to make it through the funeral and keep living for a while longer. I realised Natalie was holding my hand, helping me through the grieving process.

When Natalie knew she was going to die, I tried to reassure her it would not be long before I would be joining her as I was nearly fifty years old. I wonder whom I was trying to comfort – her or me. I began my journey of grief by being on a road of destruction. I was slowly destroying my body and mind with my poor health choices. I had stopped exercising, kept an unhealthy diet and was consuming substances which helped me achieve temporary escapism. The acute weight gain caused me to have little self-esteem. I stopped socializing with my friends and family as I preferred my own company. When I ventured out and about, I kept myself within my own world, avoiding eye contact and trivial conversation with others. I craved silence and stillness which amounted to nothingness. I could not stand the sound or vibrations of music or chatter. Life seemed unimportant, my life purpose unimportant. I was in limbo because I wanted to be with my daughter in her world while still living in this world. My mind was stuck between her and my world while I was continually reaching out to her.

The meaning of life is very different after you lose precious people in your life. Money, places, people and things are insignificant. I was irritated by people quibbling and fussing over trivial matters. Sleep – that was a hard thing to come by when I was learning to live and love again. I say 'love', because I was learning to love myself again. I had no concern over what I looked like, it was all meaningless. It probably seems inconceivable to someone who has gone under the cosmetic knife in a bid to enhance their looks to understand someone who has no care what their figure is like.

What does it take to fight back? I assume everyone has their own reasons for wanting to make their way back. I was knee-deep in a dark, suffocating swamp. When I was drunk I held my breath as long as I could, because I did not want to breathe again. I had thoughts about what way would be the best way to leave this world to enable my young son to be financially provided for, but there was none. I began thinking of the love and support my son Cameron would have to live without if I left him. The only way I could escape my pain was to take my own life, but this was not an option when Cameron needed me. If I could not avoid the pain then I had to tackle it head on. I could sidestep my grief no longer so began riding the waves for the sake of my son. Many of my friends and family told me: "Thank goodness you have Cameron!" They have no idea how true these words are.

I realised alcohol was a crutch I was leaning on too heavily, so I began putting the bottle down. When I reduced my alcohol intake and stopped taking prescription drugs, I surfaced from a desolate, dark place and was able to breathe in fresh air again. As soon as daylight hit me, so did the intense emotions of grief. My mind spun like a merrygo-round, thoughts pinged from one thing to another. No matter how much I tried, I was powerless to stop the burling. When at my worst, I stared at my washing machine, wondering: 'How do I work that?' I was always searching. My mind felt as if it was chasing after a bus it would never catch. I tried to fill the void when I went to shops and bought things I did not need, then spent more time taking them back than I did buying them. I soon understood the advice not to make any major changes in the first year of grieving after I bought and returned a car, caravan and nearly a house. I desperately needed to stop the craziness, put my feet up and slow my thoughts down, but I couldn't. I felt incompatible with human life, because I functioned at high speed, while the rest of the world dragged at a snail's pace. I became critical, impatient and irritable about the way people got in my way and slowed me down.

I tried to read books to understand the emotions racing through me. I lacked the concentration to read selfhelp books; they were too wordy and cold in meaning. Spiritual and psychic books had helped me work through grief in the past, so I kept my hands and mind busy reading them instead of working my way to the bottom of a bottle. I began thinking myself out of the gutter of despair by clinging onto the pole of hope, edging up the steps away from the gloom that had dragged me down for long enough. I realised I had to find happiness again but in a world without my daughter.

As to the beginning of the reversal of my destructive behaviour, I would probably pin-point it to a time when I was hit by an illness which gave me a glimpse of me going in the direction away from life. For months, I suffered great abdominal pain. I chose to ignore it as I did not care if I lived or died. One night, the pain was accompanied by an infection so severe it caused me to seek urgent medical treatment. It floored me, causing me to do nothing but sleep for days. I realised I did not want to be ill or unable to live my life to the full. I also suffered from recurrent headaches, and I believed that they could be linked to the abdominal condition or caused by stress. I tried to find a plausible reason for the pain.

Past Life Regression Hypnotherapy Healing

Every disease, illness or imperfection in our body usually starts with the mind, so this is what I began to work on first. I delved into the theory of Quantum physics as it demonstrates how we store our memories in every cell of our bodies rather than just the cells of our minds. It is thought that the particles in the energy part of our human form can retain memories of trauma, disease and illness throughout our lives. These memories can be retained and be present in subsequent reincarnations of our soul if they are not healed. Repercussions from these memories can trigger us to explore lessons unlearnt or they can be a clue to help us on the right path in our current life.

I am very fortunate to have a friend called Paul Williamson who is a well-travelled and extremely experienced Past Life Regression Hypnotherapist and author, trained by the famous Newton Institute. Paul previously gave me Past Life Regression sessions, one of which took me back to a life where I had the name of Sandra. This is a name I have disliked, probably because I had lain beaten to death with a broken arm. Knowledge of this trauma helped me identify the root cause of my right arm being sore in my current life, subsequently enabling it to heal. My headaches and abdominal pain were recurring regularly, so I viewed this as a sign to request a further session from Paul to see if we could identify the cause and meaning for them.

While I went into a hypnotic state, I began having severe pain in the left side and rear of my head. To my complete surprise, I identified myself as a female spy in my twenties. Originally from America, I had detached myself from my parents and family. I had been taught to be emotionally detached from people in order to carry out my mission well. I sensed that I had been given a brown uniform, but on that day I was wearing a casual outfit belonging to the 1950s era. My hair was dark-brown, plaited at each side and raised on top of my head to meet in the middle.

I was in a bright room containing large windows with wooden frames. The location of the building remains unknown to me. I could see one large desk with a male person near it and sensed there may be one other male person in the room. I was happy and carefree when I entered the room with a basket in my right hand, delivering something to one of the men in the room. It was a place I was not used to visiting so the true purpose of me being there is a mystery. My mission was cut short and incomplete due to being in the wrong place at the wrong time. I was living in war times and quicker than I could understand, the left side of the building blew in and collapsed on top of me. The left side and rear of my head took a large blow from bricks, and a wooden beam lay over the left side of my abdomen and chest, crushing and trapping me.

When the room collapsed, I felt my spirit swiftly leave my body. I saw a vision of a white interchangeable substance which I understood to be my soul, whooshing out of my body as if it had been given a vigorous swoop with a large brush, swinging from left to right and then upwards. I felt calm, safe and free as I continued higher, gathering speed as if I was being pulled towards a huge magnet. The essence of me was like a weightless white curtain with a texture similar to clean smoke or freeflowing candy floss.

I was on my own and I knew exactly where I was going. As I rose to my destination I felt as if I was in a non-constricting vacuum without walls or sides. Sprays of pulsating white sparks flowed gently around and through me, giving me a warm and powerful spiritual shower. I basked in the great love from within and around me. The higher I soared, the lighter and happier I became. All the negative debris which had been stuck to me during my earthly existence had been cleansed away. I was an entity full of life, left with a feeling of sheer delight. My spirit was like a dancing, giggling, twinkling fairy light, full of mischief and lightness. This description is the closest to explaining what the spirit of me looked and felt like as there is no earthly substance or feeling I can compare it to.

I continued to go home to the afterlife where I found myself standing to the left of my spirit guide and next to him was my dad with what appeared like a white soft linen safety curtain between us that made my view of them slightly glazed. My spirit guide had shown himself when I was studying for my Reiki Teaching Masters exam. He had been dressed in a red outfit with gold trims and a hat similar to one a bishop would wear. His attire looked regal, although in contrast it reminded me of one I have seen in a Beefeater advertisement. He had dark hair and was bouncing towards me, overjoyed for us to be saying ‘hello’. He gave me a virtual golden sash as a gift for my achievements. I am aware that the colour gold is used to protect women in childbirth, but the reasoning behind the gift remains unexplained.

My dad has always shown himself as he had looked in my current life – in the guise of my dad. This contact was very different; I was seeing him with my spirit guide as they appear in the spiritual realm. I was on their turf and they had no need to have their ‘character’ clothes on. They were like so many different characters in one but at the same time appeared like window display dummies which could portray any other character. Their spirit really did seem the same as a free hand which could fit into any glove. This was the way I tried to explain to my daughter what our spirit and body were like when I tried to help her with the thought of dying. The true essence of my dad and my spirit guide stood beside me in silence, smiling. We were in a kind of waiting room when they turned to look at me then look to their right. They were waiting for something or someone and to talk to me would spoil the surprise.

If there was an earthly way to explain what happened next, I could only describe it as if I was watching a singer walking through the smoky door on the Mathew Kelly show called ‘Stars in their Eyes.’ “Tonight, Matthew, I am going to be…..!” My dad and spirit guide stood and looked to their right for a few minutes more, until the spirit I knew as my daughter came forward, dropping down as if she had just jumped off a train from somewhere. She appeared to me for the first time not dressed as Natalie but showed herself in all her glory as a free white spirit of many souls and of many lives and yet reminded me of a clear slate. I could feel the three of them 'gelling' with each other as if they were holding hands, but they weren't. They were sharing a kind of spiritual love energy which was part of their being; it reached out and linked with me. The immense feeling of love and, most of all, the overpowering carefree and up-beat childlike happiness they all shared filled every inch of me.

I could hear Paul asking me questions about what was going on, but I just wanted to enjoy the meeting for a while longer. Paul asked what colour Natalie and I were linked to. Natalie was linked to the colour orange and I was linked to the colour blue. I stood communicating with her, my dad and my spirit guide without talking out loud. I asked what the connection was between my past life and my current life. The previous life was for me to learn about complete detachment from emotions so I could complete my mission successfully. My current life's purpose is for me to experience many deep emotions. It was thought that experiencing these opposing lives would help me find a balance between the two. Natalie told me we were a team in my past life, trying to help the people of our country. She said we are still a team in this life with a purpose to help many people. We are to do this by bringing about an understanding of the love-link energy within ourselves and with every living thing. I was to complete this task by writing the book she was helping me to write. Paul instructed me to ask if she had any advice for me while writing the book. Natalie replied: "Keep it simple and true."

After she finished speaking, we basked in a long, psychic embrace, then the four of us raced – like giggling children on an Easter-egg hunt – towards the Akashic records to check if there was evidence of us having past lives together. We found a large book on a shelf in what looked like a timeless and endless library with white marble pillars. The book was so large we could not see the top end of it when we opened it. The pages on the left side appeared to be alive with movement. I could see the colours of the Earth – green, brown and blue, wafting about like streamers in the wind – and I could feel the seasons contained within the layers. The pages on the right side were much fewer and less bulky. They were mostly white in colour and looked fresh and unwritten. I wanted to peak inside the contents of the white pages to see what was still to come in my present life and any future lives we may have together, but Natalie's spirit stood in-front of the book and snapped it shut. She giggled, turned to face me and shrieked with delight: "It's a secret!"

Natalie had one last message before my session was to end. She said: "Love always, not just for one person or one country, but love always for everyone and all countries." This was meaningful as we used to text each other by phone: 'Love you, always.' She had hoped to leave me a letter before she died, but she deteriorated too quickly. However, she managed to find a poem to give me and had signed it: 'Love you, always, from Natalie.' These few words verified how she wanted to be part of spreading the love and help give more understanding of the spirit world to everyone and to every country just as she had done in our past life together, while in her life with me and now from the spirit world. I realise I have my own 'Cheerleader' on the other side. I wonder how it is possible for me to be so proud of my daughter's achievements in her spiritual work, but I am.

Before Paul hypnotised me, I was sceptical of the intentions we had of reaching Natalie. I had had Past Life Regression sessions before so knew what to expect, but I wondered how it could be possible for me to experience being in the afterlife when I was not dead. I was aware of Paul's voice and of him sitting beside me most of the time, but it was as if I had jumped into the next room to talk to the spirit who was my daughter. Not only did I talk to her and see her as she is now, I could see and feel her in all she had ever been other than the character of my daughter. I could feel her endless smile as she seemed to jump with a childlike skip towards me. She appeared to have a busy schedule and had to be called on to come and meet me for a short while. During previous meditation sessions, I heard her tell me: "Make an appointment." This makes sense now as I could see how busy her happy spiritual life was.

The session was mind-blowing as it gave me a greater understanding of the spiritual healing energy which is part of us all. It enabled me to step forward on my journey, away from the unbearable pain of losing my daughter, knowing she is happy and doing well. Throughout my life, I have had visions of a wooden house with a lovely garden and have been unsettled in all the houses I have lived in without understanding why. I presumed my unrest was due to having so many housemoves in my life. I can settle now I understand I have been pining for a home and loved ones I detached myself from in another life.

I later asked spirit for a name in my past life to try and piece it all together. I was given 'Burgess.' Before spirit's message, I knew nothing of Guy Burgess and the Cambridge spy-ring. A further regression session would be required to find out more of my past life as an American spy, as my existence would probably not be documented.

The merging of my past and present lives provoked a road junction, a kind of goal-post which acted as a turning point or a reminder of what I had preplanned for my life. I just had to gather my thoughts and figure out what that plan was. The goal-post provided a kind of pit-stop which inspired me to think about my life and my possible future. After great thought, I realised there are times we don't know where we are going until we understand where we have been.

When people have a near-death experience or when they pass over to the other side, they talk about having a life review to work through what they did right and what they could have done better. The records of these lives are known as our Akashic records; I have seen mine so believe they are real. They exist for us all to learn from when we are on the other side. When we feel a presence in our lives it can be our loved ones around us or it can simply be that someone on the other side is delving into our records as we are living the experience. Would it not be great if we could all learn from each other by writing about our life experiences and share them before we die instead of waiting till we pass over to explore our achievements and failures? We could provide ourselves with answers at the back of our life quiz book. We might be able to pass with flying colours in our current lives instead of having to turn the page after death before we see the answers and reach our conclusions. In comparison, we could jump from mailman to manager in one huge leap.

The difficulties we do not overcome in this life may have to be conquered in subsequent lives. I had a glaring goal-post reminding me to examine my opposing lives to give me the answer to where I am supposed to be and what I am to overcome. My mind became busy wondering how I could help myself. My past life featured detachment from people so I began thinking about the attachments and emotions I have experienced in this life to find the balance between the two.

Finally, everything came crashing together and made sense. Natalie told me through Patsy I would write a book. I had known from a young age that this was one of my goals in life, but I became sceptical as I believed it would be an academic piece or a novel. I wondered what subject I would write about. Natalie told me I would write about separation and loss to help other people, but it would also help pull me back from the darker corners of grief. A heavy weight of responsibility sat on my chest at the thought of completing this huge task.

So, there I was, surrounded by peaceful stillness and dim light in the early hours, wondering how to begin the story of my life. "Keep my photo beside you," Natalie said. I tucked her photo next to me and stared into her eyes to feel her tangible love and hear her infectious laugh. Gently, I released the recliner foot rest on the sofa to raise my feet and heaved a huge sigh. I closed my eyes and let my mind wander. All that remained was for me to put pen to paper to help me find the stepping stones towards having a successful happy last chapter on Earth and to feel the love as Natalie asked me to.

THE EARLY YEARS

Childhood Days

I was born on a winter's day in 1966 in the Maternity Home of the Stirling Royal Infirmary, probably with the Supremes singing 'You keep me hanging on' on the radio or more appropriately for my life, listening to the Beach Boys bellowing out 'Good Vibrations.' My Papa Nicol stood over me while I lay in my hospital cot. He looked at my little hands clenched into tight fists and warned my dad: "Expect a determined one."

Everyone has an earliest memory of their life. Mine involves being pre-school age, dressed in a pretty camel dress coat, white bonnet with a pink ribbon, white gloves, lacy white itchy tights and shiny, black patent-leather shoes. I walked behind my mum, not happy about something as usual and threw one of my tiny white gloves over the wall next to me in defiance. Around the same time, I was dressed in the same pretty coat and was dropped off at a nursery. I might as well have been plonked on a desert island as I believed I was on my own and my mum had left me there for good. I tried to bang the closed door down and screamed intensely for my Mum. This was the first experience I had of the hurtful pain of separation. The fear of never seeing my mum again was an emotion too big for me to cope with.

I grew up with two brothers - one who is two years older called Charlie. He was named after our dad and our paternal grandfather, Papa Nicol. My younger brother David is one year younger. He was named after our maternal granddad, Papa Hamilton. I was named Helen after my maternal gran whom we called Nana. So, there I was, wedged between two siblings usually being the cat amongst the pigeons. My brothers acted as good buffers to stop me getting my own way all of the time. I shared what toys and sweets I had freely, but my determination needed a lid on the boiling pot.

Charlie was born prematurely and taken home from hospital minus his twin brother who died at three days old. My Mum was not given the opportunity to see or hold Charlie's twin or attend his funeral. In my mum's time, it was deemed to be in the best interest of all concerned to get on with life without dwelling on the separation or loss of a baby. The powerful bond parents usually have with their baby even before it is born was not considered or fully understood until more recently. The Stillbirth & Neonatal Death Charity (SANDS) helped my mum locate where her son was buried. She was able to find peace when she was permitted to acknowledge his existence and visit his grave for the first time at seventy years of age. I did not give my spirit brother much thought, until one day he came forward during a reading from one of the members of The Spiritualist Church. He contacted me to tell me how proud he was of his sister.

Home for Charlie and my parents was in a tiny flat in Causewayhead, Stirling. Later, they moved to a threebedroom flat on the first floor in St Ninians, Stirling, where I lived till the age of thirteen. I loved living in this apartment as there were hoards of other childhood friends living in the co-joined buildings containing many flats. I used to gaze out of the living room window at the miles of scenery for hours. We did not have a television for some of my childhood. My parents were able to rent a black and white one until a rented colour set took pride and place in our living room.

I was fascinated by the pretty ice patterns on the inside of my bedroom window when I opened my eyes on winter mornings. I was not enamoured by the extreme cold when I had to drag myself out of my cosy bed, though. There was no such thing as central heating in the apartments. However, I had plenty of warm blankets and regularly slept with a makeshift hot-water bottle which was an iron-bru glass bottle filled with warm water and wrapped in a towel. We had a small two-bar electric heater in our living room. It was switched on early in the morning to enable my brothers and me to run from our beds and huddle in-front of it while we got dressed for school.

Charlie made a fire of his own when he lit a match and held it under his bed to get a better view to locate his belongings. Unfortunately, the mesh under his bed instantly burst into flames. I ran through to the living room shouting "Fire, fire!" It is no wonder we were put out to play when the weather was dry, regardless if we wanted to or not.

The children who lived in the apartments played with my two brothers and me; we all grew up together. We played many group games such as Hide and Seek and Best Man Fall, and we challenged each other with a game of beds, which is a game otherwise known as hopscotch. We messed around playing with skipping ropes and chased each other. Sometimes, we would get blankets out and place them on the ground underneath the windows of the flats and play with each other's toys and board games. Occasionally, some of the parents, including my dad, took many of us children to a large park in-front of the apartments to play a game called rounders which is similar to baseball.

It was deemed safe for us to explore together, walking for miles in fields and around rivers and ponds which were lush, clean and full of life. We would return when we were hungry, clutching mementos such as flowers, tadpoles and tiny fish and – on one occasion – a frog. We played in the vast number of woods, exploring, building gang-huts and making rope swings on the trees. We had fun, innocently plundering in people's gardens or playing Chap-Door-Run.

In the winter when it snowed, we slid down the hills surrounding the flats in plastic bags, on kitchen trays or hunched over on our feet while using our hands to steady us. My dad gave us a super-fast wooden sledge with metal runners. We had the best fun flying down the hills until one day things did not go to plan. David sat behind me on the sledge while we zoomed down a hill at great speed. Our fun was cut short when we crashed into the wall of a building. David's weight forced me harder into the wall on impact, so I lay there unable to feel me legs. Luckily, there was no long-lasting damage but much to our disappointment, we never saw our fantastic sledge again.

Our summer times seemed to be much hotter than they are today. We ran around in our bathing costumes, tip-toeing in our bare feet on the burning hot pavements and jumped into communal blow-up paddling pools. When it rained, we found other pastimes to occupy us, playing in the close. This was the stairs and corridors of the flats where we played shops and other role-play games.

Sometimes, we would share each other's bikes and scooters, taking turns each to tear up and down the long pavements surrounding the flats. When I was seven years old, I flew down the hill beside my home on a small borrowed bike. The thrill of feeling the air whizzing past my face and blowing my hair around made me shriek with delight. My joy was short-lived, because my right foot got caught under the pedal. Before I knew it, I was catapulted up and over the bike and landed tooth first. I had to live with half an upper front tooth until I was eighteen, when I could have a cap fitted on-top to improve the look of my smile.

During the warmer months, we had a few holidays and days out. We enjoyed many summers camping in a large tent at Silver Sands in Lossiemouth. This was a time when it was more common for people to camp in tents rather than holiday in caravans, chalets and lodges. We enjoyed tins of soup or beans and sausages warmed on a gas stove with dried smash potatoes from a packet. We loved playing with our buckets, spades and fishing nets and jumping in and out of the sea. We snuggled in our sleeping bags at night, chasing the bugs and beasties in the sand.

Portobello outdoor bathing pool was a place many people flocked to on hot days. David was just a toddler so I could not have been much older when he managed to climb up the steep stairs of the pool's large slide at the deep end. My dad was busy talking to someone when I shouted: "Dad, dad, dad!" Wait a minute!" he said, raising his hand to stop me from talking. I interrupted him again: "Dad, David is sliding down the chute at the deep end!" Looking to where I was pointing, my dad glimpsed David as he slid down into the deep end of the pool with a gleeful expression on his face. Seeing the danger, my dad dove into the pool, rushing to reach him before the water swallowed him.

On hot weekends, hoards of families gathered at a grassy park in Dunblane called the Leigh-Hills to picnic or lie and sunbathe under the warm sun. We cooled down by swimming and messing about in the clear spring-like river. We played in the play-park playing family games of tennis and badminton or had a kick about with a ball. These were simple but great times.

My Papa Nicol drove us in his Volkswagen campervan to play in many parks, walk in woodland areas and mess about at the seaside. Sometimes, he set up a large target and taught us how to shoot arrows with a large bow. Other times he took us treasure-hunting with his two metal detectors and took great pleasure in showing us his collection of coins and treasures he found in and around the site of the Battle of Bannockburn. I loved travelling in his campervan. I promised myself I would buy one but never did. Natalie bought me a campervan ornament when she was young and said: "There! Now you have one."

I was not aware of peer pressure to keep up with fashion trends or to have the latest gadgets. I have never been interested in these things so may have overlooked them with childhood eyes. Most of the families living in the flats were not wealthy enough to follow fleeting trends. Many of the children had parents who worked full-time hours so they were latch-key kids like us. Charlie was considered to be the most responsible to carry the key of our door to let us get in and grab a quick lunch before dashing back to school and for us to get back in at the end of our school day. David and I sat on the red window ledge in the close beside our front door many times waiting for the first glimpse of Charlie with the key. He was usually late, because he hid from boys who were bullying him. The process of bullying being tackled at school seemed to be ineffective - the bullies were punished, then they sought revenge on their victim for reporting them to the teachers. It appeared to be best not to say anything and sort out our problems ourselves.

My childhood was lived in the times of the school belt. It was the kind of punishment given to us by our teachers when we misbehaved. They would throw a wooden chalk board duster at us or strike us with a belt or strip of leather which made our hands sting for hours and dented our egos for much longer. On the plus-side, children were much better behaved in schools, not that this practice should ever have been considered acceptable. Sometimes, parents would repeat the thrashing at home if they found out their child had given reason to be given the belt.

Charlie was on the receiving end of my dad's belt or sandal far too many times to be viewed as justified or appropriate punishment. When we heard our dad's unfastened 'Jingly Jesus' sandals on his feet jingling towards us we would rush to stop what we were doing. We did not want to be thrashed for being naughty or if we could not get things right at school. I am haunted by the verbal and physical abuse Charlie received when my dad chastised him to do better at school. I felt helpless, unable to stop these beatings until one day, I put my hand between Charlie and my dad's offending sandal. I expected to be reprimanded for interfering but to my surprise, my dad looked at me and ceased hitting my brother.

My heart reached out to Charlie as I knew he was being bullied at school and had to take these beatings at home. I often wonder if this was the kind of life many children of those days had to endure. Many of us of that era can remember being given lashes of the belt, but I bet the majority of us can't remember the reason for the punishment. The physical pain of any abuse can last a few hours or more, but the psychological repercussions have the potential to last a life-time.

There are family circles in which there may be individuals who have it in their nature to sexually abuse children and mine is no different. The house was quiet and the children I had been playing with were asleep in their beds. I was falling into a deep sleep while a soft light from the hallway shone through the solid glass window above the near- closed bedroom door. I was awakened by the sound of movement on the upper landing. The bedroom door slowly opened, making the room lighter. I half-opened my eyes to see a male silhouette near the bed. I didn't think too much about his reason for being in the small box-room I lay in. He came closer, put his hand under my short nightdress and was feeling the skin of my upper body. I froze. I had no idea what he was doing or why but knew it felt wrong. I did not know what to do or what to say to get him off. I was under his care and believed he had sole authority until his wife came home. He was slowing moving his hand down when a voice told me to roll over. I did as the voice instructed and rolled right over onto my right side to face the wall away from him. He immediately yanked his hand back and retreated from the room. In my half-dazed state, I was left to lie and wonder what had just happened. I was ten years old and had no knowledge of anything to do with boys, never mind anything else. I found myself in this man's company again but the details I would rather forget. I was grateful Spirit was with me, giving me advice on how to deal with the situation.

It took me to reach the age of thirty-two before I broke my silence with my Mum about him. My silence was based on the fear of being viewed as a troublemaker in the family and wondered if I would be believed. I was confused at why people are capable of doing such things and why it can be the whistle-blower who is viewed as causing the upset. "Don't tell tales" and "Don't tell lies," my dad used to say. He and I had a strong bond so I kept thinking what he might do to this man if he ever found out. I had already witnessed my dad's anger at relatives when they mistakenly left me to walk two miles home in the dark after an event when I was nine years old. Children remember more than some adults think they do. They are precious and should be treasured and encouraged to fulfil their potential, not abused.

Many memories of my school days are based on the sensations and emotions they provided. I loved attending my art classes at high school, because my teacher was inspiring, very talented and had fabulous teaching methods. One of the first lessons he gave us was to enable me to experience a strange phenomenon, but I was not to realise it for many years. He asked us to draw something from our minds. I did not like this idea but painted my picture anyway. I drew a house in an estate which was surrounded by fields and had a large red-bricked factory next to it, pouring out steam. I was advised that my picture would not be considered a good piece of art as it did not have good negative and positive shapes. With this thought in mind, I threw it away but now wish I had kept it. My picture was identical to the house and scenery where I now live, including the red-bricked factory in the next street. I was not considered a suitable candidate to attend Art College – probably because I failed to attend school during the latter years.

Due to having started school when I was four and a half years old and not wanting to stay in school education any longer than necessary, I was shoved into classes I had no intention of finishing. These were classes where a group of us waited until we were sixteen years old before we could legally leave. My friends and I occasionally hid up the 'Long Line' which was a quiet country road. A police car drove past, then reversed back to us. The police constable asked who we were and what we were up to. They left after questioning us and said we were not worth bothering about as we would not amount to anything anyway. My best friend Fiona got upset about their comment, but I couldn't stop laughing at her face of disgust. Their comment didn't make her go to school any more.

The last time I skipped school with Fiona was when there were quite a few of us hiding in her house, including boys from another school. I laughed at one of them as he was losing his patience when trying to forge a letter from his Mum to excuse his absence from school. I told him not to worry, just to try and write another one. He gave me a sarcastic look and pointed to a large pile of scrunched up bits of paper which were his numerous attempts to complete his letter. Fiona and I were long past trying to provide forged letters for our unauthorised absences. After some time, there was a knock at the door and everyone ran and hid. It turned out to be a false alarm as it was only Fiona's older sister. Her sister could not help but laugh when she went into the kitchen to find one boy trying to fit into a tiny cupboard and two boys hiding under a clear glass table. Later on, there was another knock at the door so this time we shoved the boys out onto the balcony of Fiona's flat and went to answer the door. We opened the door to find my step-dad, Bert, standing sternly. "You best get down-stairs," he said. Meanwhile, my mum was in her car, watching the boys being shoved out onto the balcony. I was made to end my friendship with Fiona that day.

Many years later, my Mum realised that Fiona had not been a bad influence on me; it was me who had normally been the leader when skipping school. I met up with Fiona many years later. We chatted and laughed about our school antics, then wished each other well and promised to meet up again another day. It has taken me a long time to realise over the years that people come into our lives to help us learn the lessons we plan before we are born and sometimes they leave us when their involvement is complete. I had to respect my mum's decision and accept the change which was to unfold in my life.

This was the first time I had an adult emotion of missing my best friend and I wanted to die. One afternoon without her friendship, I decided I had nothing left to live for. I felt so alone and could not see what there was in my life to keep me here. I realise now, looking back, that this feeling of wanting to commit suicide was real and is, perhaps, how some teenagers might feel when contemplating to end their lives. It all seems pretty trivial now but very upsetting and real to a teenager's mind.

I put on weight during my teenage years as many children do, but I had not really noticed it. It was other people who seemed to have a problem with the way I looked. Children generally put weight on before they have growth spurts and stretch taller. I often wonder whether they may not grow to the height they are supposed to if they don't first put on that puppy fat. I received unpleasant comments for a while, but I was able to brush them off. I am sure there are many children who are not so lucky. My Papa Nicol used to look at me and say: "We eat to live, not live to eat." Another family member said: "You are like a wee barrel!" Once, I heard my friend's mum ask: "How can she be a dancer - she is fat?" The worst comment was when a group of boys did not see me walking from behind an ice-cream van at school: "Aye, she's good at gymnastics, but she wobbles when she does it." There were girls around me who starved themselves to stay thin or suffered from bulimia. In response to the nasty jibes, I resorted to cutting out all the sweet and fattening things in my diet.

Teenagers, who are bullied, lose their friends or think they are ugly or fat could feel they have good reasons for not wanting to continue living. I did not get as far as thinking about how I would end my life because of losing my friend. Once I had exhausted my afternoon temper tantrum of "I have no friends, I have nothing," I picked up my dancing shoes and began thumping my emotions out of my mind and body.

My Hobby

My younger cousin began going to a dance class in an old Scout hall at the top of Queen Street in the town of Stirling. I was playing with her at her house when my aunt asked if I would like to go to the class, too. My mum took me to a ballroom-dancing class when I was five years old and I had screamed the place down because of separation anxiety. This was different, however. I loved trying to dance at home, and by then I was nine years old. When my Papa Nicol and aunt dropped me off at home I raced up the stairs, flew through the open front-door and burst into the kitchen to find my Mum arduously doing the family's washing with a twin- tub. "Mum!" I shouted, "Can I go to dance classes, it's only fifty pence?" Weeks before it, I had messed about skating at my local ice-rink and proudly booked a skating lesson for myself at five pounds an hour. I raced home to get the money for the lesson from my mum but on arrival was told where to go. Money was always tight so there was no way she was giving me five pounds that day or any other day. With this in mind, I was waiting on the answer with hope but expecting another refusal. Her answer was swift and clear: "Aye hen, fifty pence a week for the class? That would be okay, you can go to the dancing." I jumped for joy and waited impatiently for my first of many lessons the following week.

My mum told me she did not realise then how long I would continue with the classes which ended up being three times a week until I was eighteen. She had no idea of the cost for the classes, all the competitions I would enter or all the costumes I would have to have made. If she had, I am sure she would not have been so quick to allow me to go. I also had no idea I would end up spending many years in the Scout Hall Highland-dancing, tap-dancing and learning other kinds of choreographed dances to perform in the shows in and around the Central Belt of Scotland. I was regularly seen day-dreaming at bus stops waiting for a bus to take me to and from my classes while clutching my huge metal swords with hilts decorated in bright red velvet material and long red tassels. Boys at my school called me 'Wilkinson Sword.' I am not sure if this was an insult or not, but I had no interest in boys or what they said until very much later.

The Peggy MacDonald School of Dancing was a well-known dance school in the area and many girls of different ages and skill levels attended. Peggy was quite strict in her methods so we did not dare not to do what we were told when she was shouting the odds at us: "Below the knees, below the knees!" If your foot was not on your other leg below the knee she would come around and whack you with a stick to remind you. One day, a redhaired lady who helped teach us shouted at me while I was in the middle of the sailor's hornpipe dance: "Sit down, sit down!" I got really confused as to why she was asking me to sit down but dared not question her. I sat at the side of the hall wondering: W*hat have I done now?* She had to wait till the music stopped and the room full of dancers completed the dance to come over to me. She laughed as she said: "I meant to sit down more when you are doing the dance." My face was beaming... *Ground, swallow me up!*

I practised hard during the classes and at home so flew through the exams and became quite skilled, but I was never anywhere near world-champion level. I enjoyed dancing at summer workshops which were geared towards attracting American and Canadian dancers to Scotland. Some dancers toured around Scotland with their families in motor homes to compete in all the dancing competitions. The competing world can be quite serious and harsh, but I just did it for the love of it. I reached the top level I could compete in with great ease but fell away from it when I was concentrating on what I had to learn to pass my Highland-dancing teacher exam.

For months I was teaching little ones at every class I attended. While having a short break, I made a flippant remark to one of the girls in my group. I told her I was fed up paying money to teach all the time and never got a lesson myself. I continued: "I might just look for another teacher if this carries on." I forgot this girl was the daughter of a large lady who sat upstairs every week taking in the money for the classes. I should have known my words would pass quickly onto my friend's mum and then to the teacher. I thought no more about it until some time later, when I was standing in full Highland dress with my freshly steamed velvet jacket, crisp lacy white blouse and brand new tight-fitting black dance shoes. I was poised in the dance's first position, with my feet turned out at a forty-five-degree angle, arms on my hips, fists closed tight and my head held high.

The examiner was a motionless woman who appeared soulless as she looked through me rather than at me. She was sitting upright behind a small desk, with her crossed legs dressed in tan tights. Her pen was already in her hand waiting for the music to start. This signalled it was soon time for me to begin my efforts to pass my final exam. I suddenly became aware of Peggy above me on the stage. She stepped forward and bellowed: "I heard you were leaving, so you can just get out right now!" I had no intention of leaving and had forgotten all about my flippant remark. The examiner remained motionless as if she was not in the same room or had not heard any of what had just been said, a kind of detachment which stank of collaboration with Peggy's plan for me. Many emotions rolled through me - shock, sadness and disappointment - but most of all it was embarrassment which caused me to relax my pose. I lowered my head with no attempt to explain myself and climbed up the stairs of the stage past the teacher without taking a last look at her. Tears streamed down my face as I changed my clothing and walked out of the hall, down the stairs and out onto the street for the last time. I had been so happy going to her school but realised I had to accept this rejection and prepare myself for a big change. I had made quite a few friends over the years while attending those classes and would miss them.

My friendship with my closest friend Barbara was found at Peggy's classes. She is known to all as Babs. She has been present throughout my life and has been like a sister to me. It was Babs's shoulder I cried on when they took Natalie's body away to be put at rest. She had an idea of how I felt as she lost a baby girl who would have been the same age as my oldest son. Her brother David died at the age of eighteen when she was thirteen. I could never have understood the pain she was going through or how to help her at that time. She continued dancing at Peggy's school of dancing, while I braced myself to begin a new chapter somewhere else.

It never crossed my mind to give up dancing after I was thrown out of Peggy's school. I had to look for another dance school; my mum as usual sorted it out for me. She was employed as a cashier in the Head Office of the Scottish Youth Hostel and amongst other things she was responsible for calculating the wages of the staff who worked in the Youth Hostels of Scotland. Her boss was Billy Forsyth who is well-known in the Highland-dancing world. Before long, he helped my mum find a new dance school for me.

I was apprehensive about going to the Sheena MacDonald School of Dancing in Cumbernauld. However, my fear was unfounded as Sheena was expecting me and welcomed me into her class with open arms. I was glad I had the opportunity to join her classes, because she was very kind and extremely talented at teaching. My previous school was all about learning dances we performed in displays and shows and that was okay, but Sheena had a refreshing new approach to the art of dancing. She was very professional and concentrated on good techniques to enable me to reach a higher level of skill. She regularly judged at competitions all over Scotland so she knew of the faults of the Peggy MacDonald School dancers before setting eyes on me.

Our main fault was that we danced with our arms too far behind our heads. Unknown to me, this always took marks off my performance when competing. Sheena made me dance with my arms stretched out in-front of me for six months until I could learn to dance with my arms stretched above me in the right position. Finally, my arms were more like the imitation of stag's antlers as they were supposed to be. This exercise made me realise that sometimes we have to go back to go forward, up to go down and pull back or do the opposite of something to find a balance in life. I had to sit an additional exam under the Dancing Board Sheena was a member of. I flew through the two exams and became a Highland-dancing teacher when I turned eighteen years old.

After obtaining my teaching certificate I continued to attend Sheena's adult Highland-dance classes for fun and to keep fit and danced in shows in various locations with other organisations. The most memorable one was 'The Merry Widow' at the MacRobert Theatre which was performed by the Bridge of Allan Operatic Society. A group of us sang and danced well-choreographed dances for a fortnight while wearing stunning outfits. We had to dance the Can-Can dance routine twice nightly due to the regular standing ovations we received. One evening, we thought we were going to die when we heard the music drill up again for us to do the routine for the third time. In those days, I was so busy being heavily involved in my dancing and performing in shows that I did not take much notice of the sadness my mum had to live with or how my dad was feeling.

My Dad

My mum did her best for her three children. She showered us with love, taught us well and helped us to have a rosetinted-glasses view of our dad while we grew up. My parents married when my Mum was seventeen years old and expecting twins. I knew from an early age their relationship was less than ideal due to the amount of arguing going on in our house and the number of times my dad left home with his belongings in a black bag. When my mum was pregnant with me, my Papa Nicol argued with my dad: "You must love her? There is another child on the way!"

I idolised my dad, and I loved how he made people laugh when he told jokes and sang songs, marking the beat by rattling dessert spoons. I rode on the luggage rack of his push-bike with a pillow underneath me for comfort. I held on for dear life, clutching the underside of his seat with my legs splayed out slightly so I did not catch my feet in the spokes of the bike wheel. I had ridden many times on his bike so I had the art of balancing on it down to a tee while he whizzed about at great speed. I realise now how dangerous this was, especially as he cycled on main roads, and the wearing of bike helmets was not much thought of in those days.

My birth certificate states that my dad was a carpenter. Obviously, I do not remember this and neither does my mum. She tells me he was a labourer. I remember him cleaning chimneys as we had to endure many nights waiting in a car or in a rickety rackety van while my parents put advertisement leaflets through doors for him to get work. We ended up helping him with this chore. For a time, we got to enjoy free trips on trains when he worked as a cleaner with the Scottish Railway Service.

He took me to a house which was not lived in but was full of objects. I looked through hoards of records and electrical stuff until a large silver cross dolls pram grabbed my attention. I played with it at home until I told my Mum I first saw it in a place full of stuff that my dad had visited. The pram disappeared and my dad not long after. When I was older, I was told that my dad broke into people's houses, and the objects I saw may have been his stash. It took me many years to learn that he was taking illegal drugs and that he was not quite the hero I thought he was.

Many of his absences were due to him being caught for doing something illegal and being under the care of HMS prison services. As I got older, I became more aware of the fact that he was in jail. While writing a letter, my Mum warned me the prison officers would read my letter first before my dad would be allowed to have it. I got angry at this and blamed the prison officers for keeping my dad away from me. My mum made me tear up my long angry letter and write another encouraging one. For one reason or another, my brothers and I never got to visit him while he was doing his custodial sentences. When I think about family members who are separated when loved ones are doing time, I wonder if it is the guilty party or the loved ones at home who suffer more. The guilt of hurting family at home must be part of the punishment when people do wrong.

I was a teenager before my mum told us more about our dad's behaviour. On one occasion, when he was chased by the police, he ran into our flat, jumped into bed beside my mum and told her to say he had been there all night. This must have put my mum in an awkward position, because here was her husband asking her to give him an alibi but to do so would put my brothers and me at risk if she was found to be breaking the law for him. The more I heard about my dad's wrong-doing, the more I felt embarrassed about how people might view me.

The final time my parents argued was after my dad brought home a black

Labrador puppy which my brothers and I named Ebb. We had the puppy a few weeks before we heard my parents arguing about the dog amongst other things. Before long, my dad was pleading with me to leave with him as he held onto another black bag full of clothes. I felt torn as I loved both my parents but wanted to go with him. "Come on, hen", he kept saying. My mum looked at me, then told him: "She knows what side her bread is buttered on." My dad looked at me while my head was down. The situation was too confusing and painful for me. "And take that dog with you!" She shouted, as my dad walked out and closed the door behind him for the last time.

This was the day my mum, my brothers and I officially became a single-parent family. I was a teenager before I found out that my dad had often left his work with his pay packet, but most of his money never made it past our local betting shop. I wondered why these shops exist in areas where weak members of the public can gamble their earnings away. We now have worse, because there are gambling websites available at the touch of a button. Is it the gamblers or their families who suffer from such irresponsibility? I know my Papa Hamilton dug my mum out of many debt problems when my dad was around. In the long run, we were better off financially without my dad.

The divorce proceedings and the matter of custody of my brothers and me went to court when we were still young. When my mum was getting ready to attend the hearing she asked us if we wanted to see our dad. I had not seen him in such a long time so wanted to say 'yes' but thought I would let my mum down and hurt her if I said so. I understood that he was a bad influence on me with how he was living his life, so I stopped seeing him. It still hurts.

When I was around 15 years old I arranged to see him. It was a hot day so it was not unusual for him to have bare feet in his unfastened Jesus sandals. I lifted his overly dark sunglasses as I had a longing to see him fully. I tried to look into his eyes and feel the bond we shared in my childhood. I wanted to know whether he could see me and what I had become. It soon became obvious that he was trying to hide his glazed, drugged eyes from me. Even so, I can still feel the pent-up love we had for each other when we met. After a few trivial words were spoken, he told me he had to go. My time with him was too short, especially as it took three years before I saw him again. The next and last time I saw him was when I was waiting at Stirling train station for a train that would take me to catch a flight to live abroad when I was eighteen years old. I am glad he came to the train station and gave me the biggest, most memorable hug which was to last me my life-time. I am thankful he came to say good-bye as unknown to me then, it was the last time I saw him before he died.

Suicide

I did not appreciate then how sad and lonely my dad was. In Dundee, on the seventeenth of November, just before my twenty-first birthday, he took a rope and hanged himself. I was not told about his death in a timely fashion by my family or my extended family. My mum found out about his death just by chance while waiting in a shop queue. She plucked up the courage to phone me to inform me that he had left this world. I was devastated but had to play down my feelings to avoid worrying her as I was many miles away.

I can understand why my dad would feel so low and put an end to his life, because I, too, felt low when I was a teenager with no friends, and I came close to thinking about it seriously after my daughter's death. My dad ended up in Dundee, when he married a woman who was also addicted to illegal drugs. I have no idea what his reasons were, but I know he lived for his sons and daughter at one time.

There are specific people who are at great risk of committing suicide such as women who are suffering from Postnatal Depression, Veterinarians, children who are being bullied at school, people who feel unloved or disliked, grieving friends and relatives and anyone who has had to suffer too much change or loss in their life. The list is not exhaustive and it is possible that not everyone will admit to having had suicidal thoughts or tendencies. Most people, no matter what age, generally do not think about the devastation they would cause amongst their family and friends when they take their own lives.

My work colleague and friend, Katrina, lost her son by suicide. She had lost other family members but felt this was a more complex kind of grief she was experiencing. She told me that my daughter did not have a choice about leaving me, but her son did have a choice about leaving her so this made her angry. Katrina knew her son was sad, but she had been too scared to admit it being suicidal depression. She wishes now she could help others stop having negative thoughts and feelings but is not sure how she could do this. She said she had skipped around the question of her son's mental health, feeling now that this was much to her shame.

She is like many of us who have lost a child: a changed person who has less patience with trivial moaning and is less tolerant of selfishness. Hearing members of an online support group say exactly what she was feeling comforted her and made her feel she was not alone in her grief. Katrina said she had to keep reminding herself to breathe and calm her mind in the first few months. She realised that if other people had survived the pain for a year or so after their son or daughter's death then so could she. She is still trying to find a logical reason for it all.

I have been trying to think of a logical reason for my dad's poor choices in life and death. Could it be the case that he was just playing his part in the saga of life which was pre-planned for a higher purpose? I have come to terms with my dad no longer being here in the flesh, but I struggle with the thought of not having the chance to put things right between us. His ashes were scattered on the grounds of Dundee Cemetery so there is no grave for me to visit and say goodbye. I have seen, heard and sensed my dad near me since his death, so I never thought till now about needing to go to his resting place and pay my respects.

He has been around me more in his death than he was during his life. He was with me when I was having my first attempt at decorating my kitchen. I was pasting another strip of wallpaper onto the wall when I heard him tell me: "That's upside down, hen." Without thinking too much about what I heard, I answered: "Oh aye, so it is." A medium later confirmed that my dad knew I had heard him. My eldest son, came crashing down the stairs of our house screaming: "There's a man in my room!" He described my dad down to a tee, 'Jingly Jesus' sandals and all. My dad confirmed through a medium he was often around me and my family. He is only sad that he cannot hold or cuddle his grandchildren. It gave me comfort knowing he was able to enjoy being around me and my family, albeit in another way. During my Past Life Hypnotherapy Regression session, I was able to see the complex, kind and loving spirit who played my dad without the rough edges. I was mesmerised by being able to look at him and see for myself that he is so much more now.

Lately, I have been playing his song 'Bridge over Troubled Water' by Simon and Garfunkel to let me feel him close to me. He used to play it over and over when he was still living at home. The words are so fitting for his purpose in the afterlife. He is helping people who are contemplating suicide.

Now, with adult eyes, I can see his life and choices from a different angle and I realise that he must have felt desolate, stuck in a way of life without love. When I was at my lowest I heard him tell me: "You are never alone" and he finished by saying: "No-one is ever alone, you just can't see us." I acknowledged him by saying: "It sure feels as if I'm alone."

I guess that many people are out of love for themselves and other people when they get so low that they think about wrapping up their life suddenly. During a reading with my paternal Great-Gran, I was told that we have nine possible exit points where we have events in our lives when we can leave this world or stay, but suicide is generally not a pre-planned option. We cut ties suddenly and leave interactions undone and lessons for our soul and soul group unlearnt. This inevitably causes distress among loved ones who are left behind. It surprised me to learn that we may have to come back to complete all we have failed or work harder on the other side to help others after a period of re-settlement. It took my dad a long time to come to terms with what he had done and find his purpose on the other side. I certainly have had an increase in interactions with people who need the help he tries to give since writing notes for my book. I am sure my dad is as much the driving force behind what I write as Natalie is. His death inspired me to write a poem about reaching out to other people…

Friends in Need

Life has many lessons, what they are we alone will know.
Do we only learn them when we are feeling vulnerable, helpless and low?
Look around you and you will find many more standing with you –
lost, lonely and going out of their minds.
Offer your hand, embrace them and give your love.
Do it for yourself and not just for God above.
For wallowing in self-pity, staying stuck on that emotional train
has never solved anything and provides no spiritual gain.
Feeling the pain of others and drying a tear
helps put troubles into perspective, crumbles sadness and banishes fear.
Look forward to tomorrow and learn from today.
Share life together hand-in-hand, come what may.

Teenage Years

I overheard my mum saying: "There are never enough hours in the day for Helen." I think she is right. My dancing occupied a great deal of my time between the ages of fifteen to eighteen years. One night, when I was seventeen, I drove to my adult Highland-dancing class. Sheena had watched me walk up from the car park without my mum dropping me off. Travelling to Sheena's classes in Cumbernauld from my home involved driving on a fast motorway for about fifteen minutes so she looked at me, perplexed: "How did you get here?" I replied happily, proud as punch: "I drove!" Sheena sounded surprised at my answer and continued her questioning with: "Oh! When did you pass your test?" "Today!" I replied. Sheena later told me she was fretting after the class, wondering if I had got back home safely.

My mum was the first to pass her driving test. She had good reason to want to drive a car, because my dad had his licence taken away from him after being charged with a driving offence. She just needed the means to pay for the lessons. My parents used to spend money on cigarettes and smoke in the house and car. This made us and our belongings stink of stale smoke. I noticed it more when I was out of the house and amongst my friends. This helped deter me from ever smoking so it could be seen as a positive. I started breaking my mum's cigarettes into pieces so she would have fewer to smoke, until one day she gave up. This provided her with extra money to play with, and the next thing I knew she was learning to drive. She was thrilled when she passed her test, and so were we as it meant that we were taken on many days out in her fabulous second-hand car.

She began taking us places we would not otherwise have gone to. We often did not know how to get to where we were planning to go. We were hopeless at following a book map and there were no navigation systems in those days. On these occasions, my mum had to revise where we were going mid-journey, telling us where we were going was a surprise. My mum would look for a car which looked as if it was going our way. Thereafter began her motto: "Follow that car!" My mum convinced my brothers and me to start driving lessons as soon as we were old enough.

My brother Charlie passed his driving test when he was seventeen years old. He proved to be very good at teaching me – so much so that he ended up having a driving school teaching people to drive cars and HGV vehicles. He took my younger brother David and me out to practice driving many times before we sat our tests.

My brother David was a tad irresponsible when he told me that he had had driving lessons and wanted to practice. He asked if he could drive me the short distance to the chip shop after one of my dance lessons. We got into our mum's car and after going through the basics, he was soon driving on the road. On the way back, he started kangarooing the car, stopping and starting, jerking his way down the street.
"Tell me what to do!" he shouted. "I thought you have had driving lessons?" "No I haven't," he said. I was too busy laughing to keep him right. Every time I tried to take a bite out of my chip I kept missing my mouth because of his terrible driving. This was typical of David and the kind of relationship we had – full of fun and childish pranks.

My Step-dad Robert – or Bert as most of us call him – was in our lives at this point and was the last one to pass his driving test in our family. He was right when he said we were in charge of a killer machine. Great responsibility comes with being behind the wheel of a car.

Bert came into our lives with a bang. We were used to being a single-parent family so he faced quite a challenge of fitting into our tight nest. Many of our disagreements occurred during meal times. Bert's parents had been influenced by the scarcity of food during war times so Bert did not believe in wasting a single morsel of food. He would make me sit for an eternity until I ate my greens. I remained seated until he was gone then sneaked away after hiding my vegetables in the bin. He had a stand-off fight with Charlie about the amount of tomato sauce Charlie put on his plate. They argued for some time before Charlie stood up and slammed money on the table. "There! There's your fifty pence for the tomato sauce." I think Charlie was missing the point. These arguments became less and less until Bert blended into our every-day life and became very much our dad, though we still call him Robert or Bert.

Bert is a retired civil servant. He served time in the Royal Artillery so had the experience for doing his work out of the Forces. He had a full life playing darts and was a football referee for under-eighteen-year-old boys. I was never interested in football, but I loved to sit with him while football games were on the television. I wasn't watching the television, I was watching him with all his extreme emotions about the game. I was his buffer for him to tell me what the players were doing. He would put his hand out shouting: "Bum referee!" at various points in the game. Every game was wrapped up by his statement "Money is wasting the game!"

I used to drive him to many of his matches and pick him back up again. Sometimes, the matches were a good distance away so I would wait for him while I read a book, then drove him home when he was finished. My mum convinced him, as she had encouraged us, to start taking driving lessons. After he had a few lessons I took him out in the car to let him practise. I could hardly keep him right for laughing at the way he tooted his horn at other car drivers. He shook his head and hands calling them "a balloon" when it was really he himself who was in the wrong.

Bert was the one who helped me get up for work in the morning for my first job. I was a paper girl on a Sunday morning, delivering papers over a large part of St. Ninians in Stirling. I had to do the run in two rounds as the papers were double the thickness and weight due to the magazine inserts in the bulky weekend papers. I loved the smell of the early morning dew and the sounds of the early birds, and I enjoyed the stillness of the streets. I am grateful for the sensory experiences this job gave me, but I did not last long doing it. I began working in a local Spar shop working from six am till eight am before school and continued with this job for a while after I left school. I am not a morning person, so Bert had to drag me out of bed at half past five. I don't think I have ever thanked him for making sure I made it to work every morning.

I left this work to attend Clackmannan College to do a basic course in Office Skills. Office jobs were in abundance and usually the easiest for females to obtain, so I thought it would help me onto my career ladder. I next worked on a Youth Training Scheme. This involved messing around with a bunch of school leavers on the very minimum wage while learning useful skills. My life had no clear direction. My dancing was the only permanent fixture in my life as a young teenager… until boys came along.

Around the time when Fiona and I were friends, I had my first kiss on the window ledge of an old roofless cottage ruin by a softly flowing stream. Fiona was dating a boy from a group of girls and boys we hung around with and I dated his younger brother for two whole weeks. As we kissed in the picturesque scene, I noticed he tasted of milk and jam sandwiches. The euphoria of the sensation was tainted by me wondering if this was what he had for his tea. I sensed our friendship would end quickly. My suspicions were correct, because someone in the group let it slip that a younger girl had put out for him while we were dating. Let's say, she was giving him more than a kiss. When I confronted him we ended up fighting. He tried to hit me but missed, and then I unintentionally gave him an impressive black eye. His brother teased him about being beaten up by a girl. His deception put an end to my association with the group and put me off boys for a while. Fiona also cut her ties with her boyfriend, because he taunted her for giving him nothing more than a kiss. We were known as being 'tight.' It was our opinion that we just weren't that stupid.

I was pretty much a free spirit and loved to dance. I enjoyed going to a weekly disco for teenagers under eighteen years old. Near the end of one of these evenings my friends rushed me into the toilet. I sat on the large sink unit in the ladies' toilets listening to them telling me that a boy wanted me to meet him the next day. We then all rushed out of the toilet to look at the boy in question. His white trainers were all I could see of him in the dark hall. I am not sure if it was the spurring on from my friends or the excitement of meeting a strange boy which enticed me to meet him. He was not as good-looking as I had hoped, but he had a wonderful personality and made me laugh. His family had very little, but they appreciated what they had. He shared his dreams of doing better in his life. When my mum and Bert met him after a few months of us dating, they told him to go home and wash his hair. I was mortified.

He bought me a beautiful necklace I loved, but it got returned to him only a few weeks later. He came unannounced as a spectator to an ice-skating disco session and did not come over to say 'hello' to me. He stood at the side of the rink watching me zoom around the ice with my female and male friends, then left without speaking to me. Through his friend, he accused me of seeing another boy and ended our relationship. I was not dating anyone else. I wrote a letter to him explaining this and put the necklace with the letter through his letterbox. I often wonder what would have happened if he had confronted me and had an adult conversation about what he thought went on while I was with my friends, instead of making assumptions. We met three years later in a shop and said a brief 'hello'. As I turned to walk out he asked if I would go out with him again. I had to give myself a minute to think about it then replied: "I'm sorry, I'm getting married." As I watched him lower his head, I suddenly wished we had tried out our relationship more than we had.

One of the boys I was with at the ice-rink ended up being my husband when I turned eighteen years old. He was just a friend who was part of the group for a very long time, before our friendship sparked into something more. I truly loved the man I was going to marry, but Bert still stopped me before walking down the aisle of the church on my wedding day: "It's not too late to change your mind." I admired him for saying this, giving me a chance to back out even though he had already paid thousands of pounds for my wedding. My biological dad had always dreamed of walking me down the aisle on my wedding day so I had mixed feelings about it. Bert had been my dad in every sense of the word so deserved to have this honour. I think it was more as if I was holding Bert up as we walked towards my future husband. Bert still maintains that the floorboards were uneven in the church. My dad was not part of my life, but I still scanned the area outside the church for him while I posed for photos. My Papa Nicol later told me he purposely gave my dad the wrong wedding date, because he feared my dad might cause trouble.

My husband had been serving abroad with the Armed Forces for some time when we got married. I had to wait a few months before I could join him so I continued working as a secretary for a small construction company. When the MFO boxes arrived, my belongings were packed and shipped overseas. The army flight tickets arrived soon after for me to join him at our married quarters. I was so full of excitement about the new chapter in my life that I did not give much thought to my family, especially my mum, who shed many tears in the waiting room of the train station. Many family members and friends waved us off shouting "Good luck," as the train pulled away.

MARRIED LIFE

Under the Military Dome

After a train journey, followed by a bus ride to our army flight, we flew for a short while until we touched down on an army barracks air field. I looked out of the window with much excitement to see flashes of young men zapping around in small army vehicles, going in and out of army hangars and groups of men marching around. As I disembarked from the plane and touched German soil for the first time, I stepped into the military dome which was a life full of khaki green. From then on, I was known as 'Wife of…' my husband or, according to army wives, as 'Excess Baggage.' We were collected by an army coach and continued our journey to Minden, a small country town in the north of what was known as West-Germany in 1985, as the Berlin Wall was still standing.

I snatched glimpses of my new world through the coach window. I was unaccustomed to such flat land, devoid of hills and glens. Many thoughts flowed through my mind as I gazed at the miles of golden scenery which stretched to the horizons. Passing many country villages and farmland, we approached the picturesque town of Minden. We slowed down, twisting and turning around buildings as we neared what was to be our new home. The sun shone on the varying styles of houses and apartments, making them look brightly coloured, fresh and new. I was to learn later that the greater part of this lovely country had to be rebuilt after the war.

Our first home was an apartment on the ground floor of a block of two sets of flats with ten apartments in each. I requested a ground floor apartment as I hoped to keep up my dancing practice without disturbing my neighbours. On entering the flat, I dumped my suitcase in the hallway and began to look around. I was taken aback at how sparkly clean it was – I could have eaten my dinner off the laminate floor in the kitchen. The taps in the toilet twinkled in the sunlight; the glare slightly blinded me as I rushed to have my first pee. I was amused by the toilet pan which had a kind of ceramic shelf – I could inspect my outgoings before flushing if I so desired. The rooms were generous in size, with large windows we could open wide in the sweltering heat. As we were a newly married couple, we were given a fully furnished married quarter with all the basic things we would need. Most quarters were like this, because army personnel were posted to different places frequently. I stood in wonderment in the living room, looking at the square green camouflage army suite, the bright white and blue sunflower-patterned curtains and the grey laminate floor which was half-covered by a brightly speckled orange carpet. I wondered if the person who had chosen the décor for our home was someone who was colour-blind. The bedrooms were pretty much the same, but they were clean and adequately furnished for our needs.

I opened the balcony door and stepped outside to breathe in the new air and feel a different angle of the sun on my face. The first thing which struck me was how dry and hot the country was compared to Scotland. I scanned my surroundings: there were rows and rows of the same cream and orange, double- and treble-block of flats with lots of people coming and going around them. People could be heard talking in different accents. Young children played in and out of the buildings. I watched a workman zoom around cutting the grass. This garrison buzzed with activity. I felt as if I had been dropped onto a new planet, miles away from home – and yet, it reminded me of my childhood days where I grew up.

I was curious about the different accents I heard. I learned that the flats housed forces families from all over Britain. The children, otherwise known as "the soldier's brats" had a generic accent as they mixed with children from all regions of the United Kingdom. I was fascinated to hear the bilingual children switching from the English language to German. There were quite a few bilingual children, because many soldiers married local German girls.

I was surprised to hear there were a few wives who believed the local girls were only looking for a 'meal ticket for life' when they sought to hook up with British lads. It was not unheard of for a British soldier, otherwise known as a 'Squaddie,' to get a German girl pregnant and run a mile. I was friendly with one lad who had a daughter his new British wife had no knowledge of. It was hard to understand anyone who would marry a soldier and not truly love them, because army life was tough. The soldiers spent a lot of time at work and away for weeks or months on army exercises. I spent much of my married life counting the days until my husband returned from these exercises.

My husband had to work through the week and leave me to my own devices at home. I went for walks to find my way around Minden and began making friends. A few days after I had arrived in Minden, a loud siren wailed. It sounded like an air raid alarm, warning of an impending attack. I was so scared and confused that I jumped into my bedroom cupboard as I didn't know what else to do. I waited for something to happen but it didn't. Eventually, common sense kicked in and I climbed out of the cupboard unscathed. After he had stopped laughing at my antics, my husband informed me that the siren was sounded once a month to check that it worked.

There was too much change around me to begin with so I got homesick. One night, my husband came home from work to find me next to a packed suitcase. I was going home to my family and friends. He pleaded with me to stay so I gave army life another go. We messed around in the outdoor pool next to our flat in the hot evenings and he took me to the Naafi bar at the barracks at weekends to meet more of the families who were in his Regiment. I went to the bar to buy a soft drink, but the bar man laughed and refused to serve me. He told me I was not allowed to order soft drinks. If I wanted to drink there I had to order a real drink unless I had a good reason not to. From then onwards, I began drinking alcohol on our nights out and had fun doing so.

There were occasions when we would go down-town to the local pubs or travel further afield to various night clubs. One night, we had seven friends who wanted to come down-town with us after a few drinks in the Naafi bar. We had just bought a brand-new blue Nissan Micra car as it was tax-free. It was fun trying to fit nine of us into our tiny car. I think the guy who ended up in the boot had the worst experience travelling to town. I was the designated driver; I didn't avoid the bumps on the road just for the fun of it. We enjoyed going to a large disco hall in Hannover which had many bars and restaurants inside it. When we went there, plenty of single guys we called 'Singlies,' came with us. When returning home, one of our friends urgently needed to relieve himself so I stopped the car at the roadside to let him out. One second he was there and the next he had disappeared. The car was full of drunk teenagers so they did what daft youngsters would do – laughed their heads off for quite a while before it occurred to them to get out of the car to find him. It was dark, so our friend had not seen the steep embankment where he stepped forward and had ended up rolling down-hill midpee.

Working Abroad

The fun times were soon not enough, and I became bored. I needed to find my purpose in life in Minden. I managed to get a paying job with the Salvation Army driving a long, extended van called 'The Bun Wagon.' It involved selling snacks, sweets and juice to army personnel in the army barracks. The manager was sceptical of an eighteen-yearold girl driving his van around, but after I had been shadowing an older girl he was happy enough. It was hard work, but I enjoyed being out and about chatting to the lads. I spent many days selling snacks to the boys. One boy asked me out on a date. He was very persistent so I told him: "I am married." "I won't tell him," the boy said. "You just have," I replied, while pointing at my grinning husband at the back of the queue.

I loved my journey going to work on the flat land, flying past the canal on my new blue push-bike. Even though I did not wear a helmet, I felt safe while making my way to work as we did not have to cycle on the road. The pavements in Minden were divided into two halves by a continuous, thickly painted white line. The half next to the road was designated for push bikes and the inner half was for pedestrians. Bikes did not stop if you were on the cycle lane so most people stuck to the correct side of the line. My mum and Bert travelled to visit us many times. Once, when we were out walking and enjoying the warm weather, Bert suddenly got a fright and made us laugh by the dramatic way he jumped up a fair height out of the way of a push-bike which was tearing towards him. I had forgotten to tell him to keep to the inner side of the pavement!

The Salvation Army job was a stop-gap until something else came along. The something else was a position as a secretary in an admin department of the Services Sound and Vision Corporation Headquarters. It involved being one of two secretaries for a very old manager who was kind, gentle and did not say much. I was sure he always wore the same suit – he smelt as if he had died many years ago but was yet to realise it. This made me make a mental note to myself to have a shower every day and wear fresh clothing when I am old. My colleague was a female who had a square face and a harsh spiteful tongue. I had no idea why she was so nasty to me, but I overlooked her resentfulness and quietly got on with the job. There was not enough work for one person, never mind for two. She always gave the important job of typing letters with carbon copy paper behind them to me. They were letters which allowed the Managers to enter East-Germany. They had to be word-perfect with every letter and dot in the right place so the Managers would be permitted to pass through the border. I was also given the responsibility of typing and sending the end-of-the-month accounts department sales figures by fax with the same carbon copy paper. My real job was to be a fill-in person when the receptionist and other secretarial staff were absent. I got experience working in other departments and enjoyed working away from the miserable ex-army female.

After a short time, I got bored with this woman and the non-existent job so asked to be moved to the accounts department, which was full of life with targets and deadlines to meet. I was told I would be given a short trial period and if I was not any good at the job I would not be given my admin job back. In my typing class at college I had made myself learn to touch-type at a high speed, so my efforts were about to pay off. I am not sure if I was young and stupid or determined and brave during this trial period as there was not one moment I thought I would not make the grade. I enjoyed working in this department, keying accounts information into computer databases at great speed and accuracy. The girls in the office did not like the boss, but I had not experienced a problem with him. I never took sides and did not get involved when they spat in the tea they gave him every day. In time, this job came to an end as my husband and I decided to start a family. I was truly sad to leave near my due date but accepted there are times in life when we have to accept change so we can move on to something else.

Army Family Life

I looked forward to having my first baby but was lonely during the last trimester of my pregnancy, because my husband had to do a tour abroad. I was used to him working away from home but was sad about being on my own on my twenty-first birthday. I chatted to my mum on the phone, then opened a box of presents she sent me from my family and friends. I had to be focused on my life and not dwell too much on being so far away from her while I was pregnant.

My belly was so big with child I was fit to burst near the end of my confinement. Even so, we went home to our families in Scotland on a surprise visit when my husband returned from his tour. I found the ferry ride tough as I kept getting practice contractions when the waves jolted me around. I thought I was going to go into labour while out at sea. We arrived unannounced at my Papa Hamilton's house when he was cooking sausages and bacon. He was so shocked and excited to see us that he burnt the food. I can still see the huge smile on his face and feel the love shining out from him.

I tried really hard to have my baby in Scotland with my friends and family around me, but it was not to be. Eventually, sixteen days over my due date, I went into labour. I paced up and down a corridor thinking my insides were going to split apart. I soon found myself in the labour suite, watching a line of ducks waving up and down on the wallpaper to the sound of the apparatus which was giving me gas and air. I was adamant I heard a fabulous unreleased Freddy Mercury song and even went as far as to try and hum the tune to the disbelievers in the labour room. In time, I was asked if I had the urge to push. I had no urge, only agonising pain. My baby was stuck, rubbing bone on bone. I started to shout: "Get it out!" I just wanted to die, I really did. The pain was too much, and I was swinging the gas and air tubing in a circle, screaming: "This gas and air is empty, it's not working!" I was told after the event that a consultant had been flown in by helicopter to deliver my baby. When I was whisked to the theatre, someone was trying to cover my face with an oxygen mask. I fought it off until the midwife explained it was for the baby. My husband stood shocked outside in the corridor when a doctor approached him. He was asked if he had a choice would he save me or the baby.

My son Kevin came into the world quite harshly as he was indeed impacted – his shoulders were stuck fast. They pulled as I slept under a general anaesthetic. I have yet to have a full explanation of what happened during my labour and the birth of my son. I guess I will never know as BMH Rinteln Hospital where he was born was burnt to the ground recently. I must have lost a fair amount of blood, because I was very weak for some time after the birth, and I could not bear the pain of sitting down for months. The damage to Kevin's little face and head from the forceps was clear the moment I opened my eyes and saw him, but the damage to my tail end took twenty-eight years to be fully known.

I did not need to search for Kevin amongst all the other babies in the nursery. At nearly nine pounds, he lay filling his cot all wrapped up like a sausage roll, listening to music on the radio. He still likes to fall asleep wrapped around and around his quilt listening to the sound of a television or radio. I lay in my hospital bed looking at him and felt the most precious, powerful feeling of love I had ever had. I thought: *I made you*!

While I was waiting with Kevin for my husband to pick us up to go home, a midwife looked at me and made me promise to take my iron supplements regularly. Now, many years later, I understand why she was smiling so much as I now stand in this midwife's shoes watching women who have had a near miss, overwhelmed at the happy sight of seeing mother and baby going home together.

In Germany, the provision of midwives who visited new mums and babies in the community was limited, so my Mum came over with my Nana to help me care for Kevin. I can still see the two of them in my mind, sitting in the living room of my apartment, knitting cardigans for Kevin after doing all the household chores.

Having a baby very much changed the dynamics in the household and my way of life. When my husband and I went out we usually went separately. The only time we could go out together was when there were house parties and we could take Kevin with us. It also affected the decisions we made in relation to where we lived. We were given a posting to Cyprus, but with great thought we passed this opportunity over to another couple. We thought our families would miss too much of the first few years of Kevin growing up. I did not have the foresight to realise having a baby so far away from family would result in my husband going to the army bar on his own for nights out.

My brother Charlie and his wife were over on a visit, and Charlie went to the bar with my husband for a few drinks. I was furious when they were gone all night as we were supposed to be going to a large adventure park with Kevin early the next morning. My sister-in-law and I put the external wooden shutters down over the windows and locked the front-door, threatening them they were not going to get in as a punishment. My husband pleaded with us to let them in as Charlie was so drunk he hardly knew where he was. Charlie's wife slept on a chair beside him all night to keep an eye on him while my husband and I slept in our bedroom which was adjacent to the living room. During the night, a voice woke me and alerted me to check on Charlie. I opened my bedroom door to see my brother's wife fast asleep while Charlie lay on his back on my settee, bringing up full portions of chips and swallowing them back down again. The voice told me to roll him over onto his side. He woke and puked up when I did this, and his wife was woken by the retching noise. She and I could not sleep for the rest of the night, because we were worried for his safety. Charlie got up the next day, fresh as a daisy, wondering if we could go and get some breakfast.

I did not have a job when Kevin was young as it was hard work looking after a baby on my own. I had been teaching Highland-dancing at a school I set up in an army barracks in the middle of Minden town. I danced and taught right up until I gave birth but had to give it up for a few months. When I resumed teaching, I had quite a few girls in the class. I organised a few displays with the German authorities for the girls to demonstrate their skills. Our biggest event was dancing in the Rheindahlem Show. I was dancing in the display myself and wondered why I could not pick up my feet and jump as high as I usually did. A few weeks later I realised I was pregnant with my second son.

I was pregnant when we moved from Minden to live in Muelheim, a town further south in West Germany. It was a busy, dirty industrial area so I did not take to life there or the dark dingy apartment we lived in. When my husband was away on exercise, I opened the kitchen window and it became completely detached. I had to hold onto it, pull it back and jam it half-shut so that it did not fall out. It took many days before a handyman came to fix it so I felt unsafe on my own. All service personnel were warned at this time of the high security threats to our lives at home and in the barracks. I heard that a family of four were attacked in their car at a filling station. Our car registration plates were changed to be less conspicuous. We were given special mirrors to check for devices under our cars and instructions on how to keep safe. We were surrounded by German apartments in a less than desirable area so I prayed for my husband to get promoted so we could get posted out.

I wondered about what some of the German people thought of us when we could not communicate with them to explain situations like the day a handyman knocked on my door to fix the light in our windowless bathroom. What the handy man saw was a naked toddler covered in poo in the bath in a dark bathroom. What had just happened was Kevin was being potty-trained and wanted to use the potty before I put his clothes on. He had missed the potty and passed a bowel motion on the carpet. He had stood on the mess and made poo footprints on the carpet which he touched, then wiped his hands on his chest and got covered in it - all in the seconds it took for me to fetch his clothes. The door-bell rang, and I thought quickly about what to do with a less than clean baby. My solution was to put him in the bath where he would be safe and could not make any more mess until I answered the door. The handy-man made his way to the bathroom before I could stop him. On seeing Kevin, he quickly ran out of the house without fixing the light. I was miffed. We were billed for the stains on that carpet when we moved out of the apartment during our March-Out.

A March-Out was the term used for an inspection of the married quarters when married personnel left their home. It involved the serious business of cleaning an apartment to a high standard in order not to get billed for damages or to pay for someone else to clean the apartment if what you had done was not up to army standard. Army soldiers and wives soon learned how to leave an apartment gleaming from top to bottom. We were not permitted to decorate the walls or cause any damage. I wanted to argue about some of the things we were charged for during our stay in army quarters, but I had no voice. I was silenced by my husband, because for me to speak up would mean he would get into trouble with his superiors. We had to accept the judgement on each March-Out and just pay the money they wanted. We won a fridge-freezer in a raffle but were billed for an army fridge we never used. When the examiner switched on the fridge for the first time after it had been in storage it made a noise. I think he thought that we had bought our fridge-freezer because we had broken theirs.

We moved house six times in the six years we lived in married accommodation. My husband was promoted after working in Muelheim for six months so we were posted to Buende, near Minden. We were given an old apartment which was miles away from anywhere and involved me catching a bus when I went shopping. I wrote a letter to my husbands' superiors to ask for a move of home nearer to the amenities as the thought of struggling on a bus with a double buggy, two babies and shopping was too much for me. We were given a ground-floor flat I loved just before my baby was born. Kevin also loved it as he played in the park outside our door for hours on end.

Life with children was good in the army, because there were plenty of wives' clubs and activities held to encourage families to get together. My mum came over to stay near the date my baby was due. I begged her to stay longer as I experienced some mild niggles as she was leaving. My labour began the next day so we made our way to Rinteln Military Hospital, while my friend looked after Kevin. My husband sat in a corner reading a Sunday paper while I rocked gently with the contractions. This labour was the complete opposite to the one I had experienced with Kevin. It was so easy and natural. My husband was asked to put his paper down and come over beside me to watch our baby being born. Our second son Colin flew into the world and was rushed over the resusitaire machine for a few puffs of air to inflate his lungs before being placed in my arms.

The Gulf War

I was relaxing in the living room of our apartment in Buende, knitting a cardigan for Colin who was weeks old. He was asleep in his cot; two-year-old Kevin was playing with his yellow circular train track and wooden trains on the floor and my husband was sitting to the right of me while we watched a news bulletin on the television. We sat in disbelief when the news reader sternly announced my husband's Division would soon be deployed to the Gulf in support of a possible war erupting. My husband and I looked at each other. Why were we told about him going to war on television by a news reader? Surely, we should have been told by his superiors and not like this. The area surrounding the married quarters was eerily quiet with very little movement. My husband was excited about finally going to do the job he had been trained for so threw himself into all the preparations before leaving for the gulf. I was full of worry about what was going to happen to him, but I had to hide my sorrow so I would not dampen his enthusiasm. I told my mum I was going to stay in Buende with my friends, but she insisted I went home and stayed with her.

My mum travelled by bus all the way over to Germany to accompany me on the drive home with my two boys the next day. When my husband had said all his goodbyes, my mum and I packed up the car with as much of our belongings as we could and began our thousand-miles journey from Buende,West Germany, to Stirling in Scotland. I had great confidence in doing this as I had done the journey with my husband a few times. He was good at route-planning so he drew me a concise map with a diagram of the last place where I could get fuel to fill the car tank and two Gerry cans with our army fuel card before leaving Germany. My mum welcomed us with open arms into her home, even though two young babies were a drain on her energy and shattered her peace and quiet.

My husband surprised me by phoning me from the Gulf. So, there we were, chatting about what the boys were up to and how I was spending my days. The information he could give me was next to nothing, but I was just glad to hear his voice. A few minutes after he ended our conversation, an emergency announcement came over the television. My mum and I looked at each other as a news reader informed the whole of the UK that we were at war with Iraq. I am guessing my husband had been granted a phone call to his family before the war erupted.

I spent my days looking after my boys, busying myself with their daily needs, visiting friends and family at home and attending some dance classes. My brother David was making plans to join the Royal Air Force so I was glad to spend some time socializing with him while my mum babysat. I was at the local cinema with him watching the film called 'Ghost' but got overwhelmed by a section of the film where the main character passed over to the spirit world. This made me think about losing my husband so I had to leave the picture hall to compose myself. My life was in limbo. I counted the days, praying for an end to the conflict so I could have my husband back and my boys could have their dad at home. The army arranged for me to be filmed with my boys in Glasgow so the clip could be sent to my husband in the Gulf. Our family and friends sent my husband letters and parcels of provisions and treats. Many people in Britain sent soldiers letters and gifts. I got upset about strange women writing to my husband but all the men got letters of support and encouragement.

I learned about the end of the war in the same way I learned about the start of it. My husband was coming home by flight and train and we had planned for me to meet him at the train station. Little determined Kevin pulled on his Wellington boots and put his tiny rucksack on his back. He was adamant, saying: "I'm going to get dad." We had no idea how he knew where I was going as we purposely did not tell him about his dad's homecoming. My husband was driven to my mum's house where he was welcomed by the sight of a large banner displaying 'Welcome Home.' Colin was only six weeks old when my husband left to defend our country in a war. Tears streamed down his face when I pointed to a cheeky little runaway toddler tearing down the hill: "There's Colin!" We had a party to celebrate my husband being home safe and sound. We rekindled our marriage after he placed a beautiful unique gold chain from Iraq around my neck. It was not long before we drove back to Germany for him to continue his work in Buende.

We had to move out of our apartment when we returned from Scotland due to a large crack which had appeared on the internal living room wall. We were housed next door to my friend Claudia, who was born in Germany. Our friendship had waned probably due to me going home to Britain throughout the Gulf conflict. She said the garrison was like a ghost town when all the British wives left. I will always be thankful for the temporary job she got me in a German factory. I enjoyed being amongst the German girls who made me feel welcome. I gained an insight into how the local people lived their lives rather than being solely confined to the dome of the British army garrison. I learnt a little German at night school in one of the barracks, but the job made me pick up a little bit more of the language to get me by.

After we settled back into army life, I found a job working in the Naafi canteen but after a day realised I hated the job of cooking and making sandwiches. My low wages hardly paid for the child-minding fees so I only lasted one week there. My childminder and I became good friends so we had many hours of adult chat while her two boys played with my boys. Life was good again; we enjoyed the long hot days messing about in our garden. We held barbeque parties where people would turn up at our house with some meat and a 'yellow handbag' or with other assortments of alcohol and we were invited to many of their parties. I have no idea why these boxes of beer were called 'yellow handbags' as they were packs of 6 German beers in orange cardboard crate-like boxes with handles. Nobody seemed to mind the loud music being played, because most people around were unofficially invited. I had the life of Riley, full of fun and laughter with very little responsibility. When I visited Scotland on holiday, I thought the people there seemed to have harsh lives but appeared to be rich with experiences. I looked up into the air and thought: *my life feels empty without purpose. It's too easy, like there is something missing. I want to live a little*. How crazy does this thought sound now? I wonder if this silent prayer is the reason my easy life turned upside down.

It did not take long for some soldiers to show their anger and frustrations which stemmed from the stress of being involved in traumatic situations while trying to help people who were caught up in the war in the Gulf. They began talking about their experiences, but only in bits. I heard about a family just like ours who were killed in a car in 'Death Valley' when they tried to escape the fighting. I had a conversation with my husband before he left for the Gulf, asking him how the Americans would know it was him on the ground and not the enemy. I wonder if I had an inkling this confusion would happen as my husband was in the row of tanks the

American army mistakenly bombed. A wedge began forming between us as he began spending more time at work and less at home.

The army had been employing female soldiers in separate divisions for many years but began integrating them into male dominate regiments. When they arrived in my husband's regiment, I discussed it with my husband. I believed it could facilitate infidelity in the ranks, especially as there were so many deployments lasting months or years at a time. I was aware of a few cases of infidelity and wifeswapping amongst single and married personnel. It proved to be a challenging way of life, because I had to mind my own business and accept this was how some soldiers behaved. I was pestered by a married soldier until our neighbour told him to lay off me. It was hard spending time with one of my friends as I knew that her husband was having a long-term affair with another married woman. During one of our house parties, a married female neighbour went out to a car in the car park with one of the single soldiers and returned an hour or so later. A few hours later, she took another married man home with her.

My husband and I had our own problems. It was not long before the jigsaw puzzle pieces of my married life flipped and rushed together to show me a whole different darker picture to the one I had idolised and lived by. The flip-side of our relationship had been there in the back of my mind, but I always chose to see the brighter side. I began making plans to move with my sons back home to Scotland to be with my parents and friends. My marriage hung by a thread and the silence and refusal to discuss our problems denied it a needle to sew it back together. My emotional detachment from my husband made it easy for me to board a ferry with my sons and reach home to move into my mum's two-bedroom bungalow with my mum and Bert to await a council house to start my life over.

Return to Civilian Life

I expect my family were happy to have me and the boys at home instead of us being so far away. I certainly enjoyed being free to live my life as I wished without the confinement and restrictions of army life. My husband had decided to follow us home after he completed his prerelease course which was designed to help him settle back into civilian life again. Army personnel were given priority when they were classed as homeless and needed to be rehoused. I had made sure I was on the council list as soon as I got married in preparation for when we would leave army life. My mum and I drove around Stirling, hunting out all the empty council houses when my application was jumped to the top of the list. Somehow, I knew a house at the top of a hill would be mine. I went to pick up the keys from the council office and overheard a man shouting at the lady behind the counter. He was arguing why my house should have been given to him because of his family's circumstances. I quickly grabbed the keys and ran out of there, leaving the man to argue his case.

There was a certain amount of excitement when I walked through the door of my new home but it smelt awful. It was in a poor state as the previous occupant was old and frail. I was given a small grant to buy materials to renovate the house to a liveable standard. My mum, Bert and I got to work stripping the whole house out. Charlie had been a joiner for a few years so he took out the old units in my kitchen and fitted a new kitchen for me. My husband arrived when all the work was done so began his search to look for work. Kevin was already attending a day nursery and Colin was looked after by his childminder called Lena when I was at work.

I had already begun a new job by the time my husband joined us. An advertisement in a free local newspaper offered employment to people who enjoyed the arts. Better still, the job offered to pay the successful candidates their child care costs. The two-year work experience drama course at Top of The Town Enterprises (TOTE) was funded by the European Social Fund. For two summers I dressed up and talked about my life as a sixteenth-century character to the tourists in and around Stirling Castle, and the two winters were spent studying academic subjects at college.

A group of us began researching a sixteenth-century character for ourselves with the help of a historian who worked with us for a while. I decided I would have the character of a kitchen maid at Stirling Castle. I chose the appropriate name of Isobel and wore a plain blue dress, white blouse, white apron and at times, a white hat. I had great fun playing this character, especially when I climbed on a tourist bus and made the tourists laugh while I was mucking about with the men, telling them I was going to stow away with them. This character allowed me to go in and out of Stirling Castle as much as I wanted. I was so used to wearing the outfit, I sometimes forgot I was wearing it and wondered what people were looking at.

My school friend Gordon decided to play the character of a jester. He was good playing this role as he used to act like the class clown making us all laugh. Another tall man chose to be a medicine man with a large black cloak and long walking stick. He was a traveller who sold his 'Magic Elixir,' his potions of medicine to cure all illnesses. He did a mini-show everyday with the jester to show the tourists how his medicines miraculously cured people from broken bones and diseases. One girl played the character of the town's herbalist. She wore a lovely pink dress and walked around with a basket full of herbs curing tourist of all their ailments. She had a part in the mini-play. She argued with the medicine man, saying her methods were better than his as his potions were just water. On older lady dressed up as a wife of a stall man who sold fabric at the market. I really liked the character of a jolly guy who played the town crier. He would go around shouting "Hear ye, hear ye," as he announced the daily events to the tourists. He had such a good sense of humour, I think he laughed his way through the two-year course with the jester and kept us all laughing with him. There were royal characters dressed in elegant regal costumes. These characters took part in daily shows for the tourists inside the castle halls. I dressed up in a fancy burgundy dress and hat I made and played music to enable the characters in the show to demonstrate a sixteenth-century dance.

As part of our training we were given instruments people of this era would have played. I took to an authentic recorder, one of the men played the mandolin and another man played a drum. I had to learn to play quite a few sixteenth-century tunes reasonably well before I could go out into the street to play them. All the characters were involved in a daily play session called 'Merry-Making' at the Stirling Castle esplanade and inside the castle grounds. We encouraged tourists to play sixteenth-century games with us. We played music for the characters and tourists to dance around in a kind of follow-the-leader snake-pattern dance. We were all filmed on the 'Wish You Were Here' television programme which was hosted by Carol Smiley to advertise holidays in Stirling. I lead the festivities, so for fun asked Carol Smiley to join in with our sack race but they failed to televise that part.

I am only realising now how well-researched and organised this entertainment was for tourists who visited Stirling. The film 'Braveheart' starring Mel Gibson had been viewed by many and the statistics showed this film increased tourism in Stirling tenfold. In the second year of the drama course, I was given the chance to perform a monologue as a kitchen wench in the Castle halls. After this monologue, I did a script about the 'Green Lady' which was about a ghost of the Castle. I got stage fright the first time I did this lengthy and complicated script. My manager, Kate Donne, who is a life-coach, actress, singer, musician and author, was flapping her fringe about as she usually did when she was worried about something. I felt guilty at messing up the performance so apologised for making her fret so much. She looked at me and smiled: "It's not that!" As soon as she spoke I heard Spirit clearly say to me: "Tell her it will be okay." I did as Spirit asked and relayed these words to her. I got a sense of what was wrong in her private life but never knew for sure so hoped she would take the message of reassurance from 'them upstairs' anyway.

My colleagues and I performed at a few events around Scotland to celebrate the Anniversary of Robert Burns for a few weekends. We were dressed in our costumes singing Burns songs, performing in shows and telling stories about his work. We were to travel to Arran to perform, but we missed the first ferry over. I was partly to blame as I had been on a heavy night out with my husband and our family. When we got to Arran, the leader of the group informed me that I was to drive the van to the end of the parade to collect everyone. I told the leader that no-one had told me I would be driving and that I was not fit to drive and anyway, what was this parade all about? He did not tell us we were to walk a few miles in a parade. He laughed at our shocked faces. So, there I was, exhausted, sobering up as I trudged slowly for miles with my colleague banging an Irish bodhran which was killing my head. When we finally reached the end and found a pub for the guys to have a pint, I asked the leader if he could get me a large glass of water while I went to the toilet to die.

We ended the summer tour in style by visiting Ayr beach. It must have been a fabulous sight watching a large bunch of Burns-like characters paddling in the sea. The leader of the troop thought it would be funny to jump on a couple of guys and soak them from head to foot. I was laughing until he jumped on me. Just before he ducked me under the water, I shouted: "No, no!" I was trying to tell him I had my character shoes in my hands. After we arrived back at the office, I heard the Manager asking the leader where one of her specially made sixteenth- century replica shoes were and had to smile when he told her: "It was floating out to sea." She thought he was joking, but he wasn't.

The first serious acting work I did was when I played Morag in the play 'When I was a girl I used to scream and shout.' I learnt my lines inside out as this play skipped back and forth in time and involved a fair bit of dialogue with emotional scenes. During my performance, I was jolted for a second when the audience suddenly laughed at what I was saying. I was totally unaware of the audience due to being so deep into my character role. The experience I had with this play is very much like when I go about my daily human life and am nudged out of my limited thinking by the voice of Spirit giving me a message or a warning, reminding me even though I am not aware of them, they are still there. I took my son's spinning top as a prop to the rehearsals at the Stirling Tolbooth which is an old haunted Jail House. While we were sitting on the floor running through our lines the spinning top began spinning on its own.

We did a few one-off gigs such as one at the Headquarters of Apple in Glasgow. We were to pose as employees of the business and attend a seminar they were holding. We were to ask the Manager awkward questions in-front of the other employees to embarrass him. The reason of the occasion escapes me; it may have been the Manager's Birthday or a big Anniversary of the company. They had a party we were not invited to, but I did get the pleasure of driving a hired top-of-the-range swish car to look the part. It made a change from driving the small basic hired cars and vans I usually drove for TOTE.

Another one-off gig was when we appeared on television in an episode of Blue Peter. We were dressed in our character clothes and were taken underground to Mary King's Close in Edinburgh. This is an underground city where many plague victims were purposely trapped when the streets were bricked up to encase them until they died. We were to act as ghosts of the plague victims and were filmed in and around the street improvising the theme of being ill, then being trapped underground. It was eerie and sad to see a doll in a corner of the street. It was left to comfort the ghost of a young child who had been trapped and died there. As with most productions, we were filmed all day, but only a small clip was shown on the programme. I was not visibly shown on television, but my shadow and my heckling were televised. I was over the moon when I was presented with a Blue Peter badge as I had always wanted one but ironically, I never got to use it.

The funniest time we had while doing a gig was when we were used for a pilot film at Doune Castle. We were to be filmed from mid-day till late at night while wearing sixteenth-century gentry clothing. We ate a huge nosh-up from the mobile film canteen before the director told us our part in the film would involve sitting at a banquet table eating and being jolly. We were already stuffed so couldn't stop laughing at each other's faces when we tried to put more food into our mouths. I am guessing that pilot film probably bombed. Another film I am sure failed involved a group of us running around Stirling Castle throughout the night while being soaked by a water hose to mimic rain, shouting: "Burn the witch!" This is an experience I'd rather forget.

I continued working for TOTE on a part-time basis. I still had no clear goal in my life so I opted to study an HNC in Computer programming and completed the twoyear-long course. Near the end of the course, my husband and I decided to try and rekindle our marriage again. We did this by planning to have another baby. Within a few weeks I ran over to my friend Liz's house to show her the positive pregnancy test in my hand. We both sat in silence as she knew about the problems I had been having at home.

My daughter seemed to bring happiness back into my marriage for a year or so after her birth. On the surface, we were a happy family once more, going on days out and enjoying holidays at places like 'Butlins' in Ayr. I am unsure when my husband and I began drifting apart, living separate lives. He would work through the week and be working away from home many weekends. I worked parttime in office jobs while the boys were at school and Natalie went to a childminder she called 'My Cathy.' My mum babysat some evenings and weekends to allow me to continue working as a dancer and actress.

Murder Mysteries

I was five months pregnant when I last did a show for TOTE but began working for them again six weeks after Natalie was born. Murder Mysteries were in great demand in many hotels all over Scotland so I was involved in shows at different locations on a regular basis. We improvised from a framework of a variety of themes with a few alternative endings. We would pre-plan what ending we were going to go by and adjust it according to how the nights' events were going.

My favourite was the Palmist Murder Mystery in which I played the palmist. I went around the guests, telling them their fortunes and wrote a list of names of those wishing private readings later in the evening. I was reading people's palms as part of the plot but surprised myself by how accurate some of the information was. I seemed to know things about the guests and even got some information about their future. As part of the plan, I was to be murdered during a private reading by one of the people on the list and the guests were to try and guess who the murderer was. This theme involved the rest of the cast wearing normal clothes and not being obvious to the punters till much later in the night. I had to keep a straight face while I was being murdered off when I heard a lady in the dining room shout: "No, she can't be dead. I really wanted a private reading!"

When I lay 'dead' in the stairway, a colleague guarded over me to make sure nothing inappropriate happened to me while I lay still. One night, I had the wrong colleague guarding me. He let some of the guests do some things they shouldn't because he thought it was funny. Another time, I had to keep a straight dead face when a guest of the hotel tried to help me. He was unaware of the Murder Mystery evening going on so my colleague had to stop him from phoning an ambulance. I must have been very good at being dead or rubbish at acting, because I normally was the one who got killed off.

A memorable Murder Mystery I was involved in was held one Christmas Eve. I drove with one of my colleagues many miles up to Newtonmore. The Santa Claus framework was new and untried. As we worked through it, we found it was too sparse for us to improvise from. My colleague, Ross, who was new to our group, ended up annoying the guests by repeatedly bantering "Ho, ho, ho!" while he mingled with the guests in a Santa suit. We never used the Santa Murder Mystery framework again and – thankfully – the hotel manager forgave the poor entertainment as he was happy with all the other regular events we did there.

We drove home at great speed as we wanted to be home for Christmas. It was extremely dark on the road due to the lights being switched off at that special time of year. I realised too late that I was approaching the end of the carriageway too fast. I scanned the road to my left, to my right then straight ahead. I thought about ramming around and straight over the roundabout but a car trundled in-front of me preventing me from doing so. I had no choice but to try and break. What happened next was not an earthly experience. It felt as if someone had lifted me out of my body, slipped into my skin and took over the controls of the car. I seemed to watch the whole scene in slow motion, in an altered time frame, from my rear-view mirror. The car was spinning around and around. Ross held on for dear life to the window on his left and onto the driver's seat on his right. I came back into my skin when the car eventually stopped. I took a minute to compose myself then asked Ross if he was okay. He nodded and stated: "That's the closest I have come to being in a serious accident." I looked at him and replied: "I was not driving the car there." No more was said, so we carried on our way till we reached home to enjoy Christmas with our families. I guess I used up one of my nine exit points of life that night.

We travelled a great deal to perform in shows, the furthest being in the south of England. TOTE arranged for us to perform a 'mini' Highland Games and then an evening show for a Business Corporation. It involved driving the long distance in a mini-bus using automatic controls. So, there we were - me, another female and a bunch of guys whizzing down to England with me and another group member taking turns to drive. The group were rehearsing their lines and warming up by rhyming "Mo Mey Me Mo Moo."

We stopped over at a cheap hotel near where our event was to take place. The evening meal was a quiet and uneventful occasion. All the guys paired off in their usual pairs when we had a Murder Mystery sleep-over. Sleepovers were events when the guests had their suspicions discussed over breakfast before being given the information regarding the killer and method used. I usually shared with my female colleague, but her boyfriend was part of our team that night. She insisted on sharing with him so left me in the hall staring at a man I had only just met.

I left it as late as possible to go to bed so I could get to know him over drinks in the bar of the hotel. I have no memory of what we chatted about but ended up comfortable at the thought of sharing a room with him by the end the night. I climbed into my bed and lay awake waiting for him to fall asleep in his. I was afraid he would hear me snore so I kept awake while I waited and waited, but he didn't go to sleep. All night, I felt an intensifying magnetic pull towards him. The room felt as if there was an electric current igniting my emotions and switching my libido to hyper mode. It took great effort not to go near him or look in his direction. I had been with one sexual partner all my life, but my marriage was over. I began talking to him by telling him I could not sleep. Before long, we were rolling about the sheets in a hotel room, miles from home.

On the morning of our Highland Games it was hard for me to keep a straight face. I think the whole group guessed what had gone on. My new friend laughed when the waiter at breakfast asked us: "How do you like your eggs?" We met many times after this, but circumstances kept us from making any more of the electric spark we had between us. Spirit can help bring people together by encircling cords around them. Each cord entwines and connects two people together for them to have either a long relationship together or a brief encounter. These encounters can be intimate or platonic relationships and for reasons which are sometimes beyond our scope of understanding. I believe we have deep connections with people we feel close to - like soul mates – but are not meant to stay with so we can learn other lessons in life. I accepted this to be true with this man.

Our 'mini' Highland Games was a success with the guys hosting the competitions and games with the guests, and I danced to a piper playing the bagpipes. We got a break at tea time to eat and practice for the evening show. Due to the severe lack of sleep the night before, I got cranky at the group for messing around and going in and out of the mini-bus for no reason. We were to travel back home after the evening show and I was to do most of the driving. I knew my lines of a monologue I was to perform and the dances I was to do, so I did not need to practice my part in the show. I asked the guys to leave the mini-bus so I could jump in and get some shut-eye.

It was very late when we headed back up north. My new friend travelled in the front of the van with me, taking it in turns to drive. We kept each other awake by chatting while the rest of the group dozed in the back. We were making good time when I was stopped by a policewoman and policeman. I pulled the van over and got out to speak to them. So, there I was, at the side of the road in England, a long way from home with a bunch of guys peering out the window. The policewoman asked: "Why were you pressing your brakes when going around corners?" I looked at her, bemused and thinking: *Is this a trick question? Was she trying to get me to admit I was going too fast?* I replied: "To slow down." After a short silence, she asked me who I was, where I was from and our reason for being on the road so late. The police constables kept me at the side of the road for quite a while. Eventually, without saying much more she signalled for us to continue on our journey. "Keep your speed down!" she shouted as I climbed into the mini-bus. I am guessing the paper work was too much for them to bother giving me much more than a caution, especially as it was a hired bus from across the border.

I had been singing, dancing and acting part-time for TOTE for many years, even though I was employed in other kinds of work at the same time. I began working for other acting companies at night and weekends. Some of them had left TOTE after being thrown out for industrial espionage and for stealing their regular gigs. They were writing their own murder mystery plots so it inspired me to write some. A Hotel called The Golden Lion in Stirling previously hired TOTE to do their gigs. The hotel manager sat beside me and another female member of the group after I had finished a dancing gig for him. He knew I performed in Murder Mysteries as he had seen me do a few in his hotel. He asked if I knew of another good company who would be interested in doing regular gigs in his hotel. I told him I worked for TOTE and they would be happy to do it, but he said he did not want to deal with them again. I have no idea why he was not willing to hire TOTE. They were happy to work with the group members so I guessed it must have been a problem the hotel had with the manager or the non-acting staff of TOTE. When I spoke to some of the other members of TOTE who had set up their own companies, they said they would not touch it as it was too near TOTE; they feared they would be found out.

I am guessing TOTE got wind of the conversation the manager had with me through the other female team member who was with me that night. The manager of TOTE and her script writer took me aside and accused me of trying to set up my own company and stealing their gigs. Ironically, I was one of the few who were not branching out on my own. I tried to reason with them and was actually surprised they thought I had the ability and time to have my own company. No amount of pleading would convince them otherwise. This was a 'deja-vu' from my dancing days. Rather than tell the TOTE manager about all the other members of the group who were pinching her work, I put my hands up in despair as I was thrown out of the company for something I had not done. I find comfort in the thought that sometimes we are meant to take a certain route in life, and if we don't take that route, we are pushed. I guessed this was one of these nudges to make me follow a different path.

The Stirling Highland Dancers

There were other jobs I was doing at this time so it was not a big blow for me to lose work with TOTE, but I missed the group and the fun times. I was viewed as an undesirable risk by the other members who were secretly stealing TOTE's gigs so was not included in their events either. I had been paid to dance from a young age at many venues in Scotland. By word of mouth I was asked to dance at many more events. I was not answerable to anyone so began combining my dancing and acting performances.

The funniest memory I have of dancing with a piper was when I was dancing with Stuart Cassells. Stuart is younger than me, full of mischief and is extremely talented. He could rattle the pipes like no other piper I knew. We worked for a tour organiser called Chick at many hotels, including The King Robert Hotel in Bannockburn, The Three Kings and The Underwood Lock House in Falkirk for weekly gigs. We performed for tourists who travelled with well-known touring bus companies like Urquharts. I danced with swords which had high hilts for me to jump over and Stuart knew this. He thought it would be funny to pipe the sword dance tune faster and faster until I found it really difficult to clear them in time. I gave him a look and he returned my glare with a cheeky grin.

A few Managers told me I was hired by a lot of companies as I was known as being a performer, not just a dancer. One evening, I had a pleasant experience with Stuart when – as usual – I asked the guests who would like to get up and dance with me. I was surprised when a seventy-year-old lady got up and stood by us. She told me she lived in America but was born in Scotland and used to be a Highland dancer. The trip she was on was one her family had clubbed together to bring her on so she could visit her homeland for the last time. I danced with this inspiring lady while she danced her last Highland fling in Scotland with Stuart piping. I knew Stuart would go a long way so was not surprised when he became famous after he founded 'The Red Hot Chilli Pipers' band.

The piper who went to the English gig with us was Alan Prentice. He is a piper who has become a good friend of mine over the years. He laughs when I remind him of when I phoned him to ask if he would come with me to pipe in England. The piper who was supposed to go with me had cancelled. I phoned Alan and asked him politely: "How would you like to join me in a wee trip?" He asked me all the details and said he would love to come. Then he asked: "When do you need me?" I replied: "Now!" He was in the middle of eating his dinner so had to put his fork down to get ready and drive like a mad-man to reach us before we left.

HEAVENLY MESSAGE

Our dancing and piping relationship began with the Stirling Touring and Guiding Services Company (STAGS). We became quite close to Barbara and Fiona who owned and ran the company. We are the original Stirling Highland Hotel dancing Duo and employees of STAGS as Alan piped and I danced every week at the Stirling Highland Hotel for people who attended seminars there. Eventually, the group progressed to three dancers and Alan piping every Thursday night with a dozen dancers on standby if our group had other events on. I had the pleasure of dancing for Gene Kelly's wife Patricia at this venue, when she was there promoting Gene's legacy. We got chatting about the book she was writing about Gene's life and work and became friends when she attended a Birthday party with my friend Lorna and me.

Alan and I were invited to STAGS tenth anniversary, where we were both presented with a small token of a stag kilt pin, and I presented them with a photo of Alan and all the dancers who were working for them at that time. Sadly, Fiona died of a brain tumour shortly after this party so Barbara had to run the company on her own. I was also working as a secretary with STAGS at that time so was shocked at Fiona's death. I continued to dance at many weekly venues and Hogmanay parties for the company, especially events in the Business Centre at The University of Stirling.

Alan tells me the most memorable gig we did together was when we performed at the Golden Lion in February 2004 for members of the Conservative Party. I danced all the usual dances, then - later in the evening - I asked Alan to join me on the stage. I was dressed as Kate O' Shanter and came into the large hall singing 'Ae fond Kiss,' while pretending to be cleaning up. With a broom, I brushed the floor from side to side and around the guests. One of the well-known politicians had books and paperwork beside her chair, so I gave her a stern look for being messy and picked them up. The audience laughed. I continued singing and brushing until I climbed the stairs of the stage. I put the brush away and called out: "Tam, Tam!" In response, Alan sheepishly crawled onto the stage and sat on a chair facing the audience, bewildered as to what was coming next. I bellowed out my monologue to the audience and at Alan. He was taken aback, because he had never seen this performance or me doing anything like it. The audience applauded, giving us both a standing ovation. We spent the rest of the evening having a meal with some of the members of the party. During the meal, Alan said that he felt like a dummy on the stage, but I thought he did well. He said: "I saw a new aspect of you." I just looked at him and smiled and hoped he had had his knees together on the stage as he was wearing his kilt.

The craziest event we did was when Alan, a few dancers and myself flew to Norway to represent Scotland in a few shows. We met up for practice sessions before the event to rehearse the traditional dances and some new choreographed ones. We had to trust the airline with all our expensive belongings. The Manager of the event and her husband picked us up in a tiny mini-bus, which was inadequate to carry all our suitcases and equipment. I thought it was funny watching them trying to squash us in around the luggage. They managed to shut the door with us all inside and travelled a few miles from the airport when there was a loud bang. We all looked at each other as we watched the Manager and her husband get out of the mini-bus to inspect the extent of their burst tyre. We had to wait until other members of the event came and loaded us all into another van which could take the combined weight of us all and our luggage.

We performed in a few shows without any hitches. There were groups from all over, but the Russian dancers interested us the most. They had amazing dance routines and colourful costumes. On the night of the last performance, we were given a hall in our Hotel to enjoy having a party with the other members of the show. None of us could speak any of their languages but most of them spoke a little English. No alcohol was allowed in the hall and there was no music arranged for us so we all made our own entertainment. We had fun singing Scottish songs and taught our new friends British games. Our fellow show folk from different countries taught us their songs with the help of a member of one of the groups who played the piano in the hall. Someone slipped alcohol into all the plastic drinking cups. It was strange having to put up with people smoking indoors, because Britain had banned this behaviour some time before this. Everyone was having a ball. We didn't want the fun to end at midnight, when the Hotel owners asked us to retire to our rooms.

We invited some of the members of the foreign groups to come and join us. Somehow, more people ended up crammed into our three-bedded room than should be possible. Alan was playing a drinking game in the corner of the room with a lot of people. They banged the floor to a rhyme and when they were caught out they had to swig a drink. We kept asking everyone to keep the noise down, but they kept on banging and laughing louder. I am surprised the Hotel owner did not come to our room to break up the party. I was happy sipping a drink on my bed while my two dancing friends played a game, drinking and swigging Russian vodka and lemon with two Russian boys they had taken a shine to. One of my friends disappeared with a boy but soon came back in the boy's arms, unable to stand up. It was a strange but exceptionally great night, an experience I am glad I had. We had to stop the van a few times on the way to the airport to allow our friend to throw up. I was intrigued as I had heard about someone turning green, but it was the first time I had ever seen anyone with green cheeks.

I had been on a drinking spree with these two dancing pals a few times as we were known as the A-Team. Alan usually gave us first dibs on taking on his gigs as we seemed to work well in our performances with him. The most memorable one was when we went to Fort William to do a display at a large outdoor show. We had to resort to changing our costumes in the car as the tent we were given had male members in it, ogling us. We had to work hard to give a good show as we had been out drinking the night before. My drunken friend at the event in Norway and at this event was jumping high, doing impressive leaps with her legs wide apart in a kind of splits position high in the air. I had to ask her to calm down as we had many more dances to perform and would not last the pace. She laughed and said she seemed to feel better when she was dancing high. I wondered how on earth she could dance like that. I thought *she must still be full of alcohol.* The announcer kept announcing when we were going onto the stage: "And here are the girls from Stirling, who drank the tug- of-war team under the table!"

The night before the event, we stayed in what looked like a normal three-bedroom council house in a normal council housing scheme. The owner of the house had converted her upstairs bedrooms into accommodation for bed and breakfast guests. She advised us that there were big parties in all the pubs as it was carnival time in the village. She said her front-door would be open and there was no curfew time we had to be back by. My two dancing friends and I sat and had a couple of alcoholic drinks while we chatted and got ready to go down the street to the village pubs. After a couple more drinks, my friend banned me from having any more as she realised I was a lightweight and could not handle much alcohol. We went and ate a meal before we went on a pub crawl. As the night went on, I sobered up while my two friends got more inebriated with a large bunch of guys. I think we ended up with a guy each walking us home. I learned the next day that my guy was from Australia and was touring Scotland in his small motor home. I wondered if I was more interested in his motor home than I was in him. My drunkest friend somehow ended up in a bush during a fall, taking her chosen guy in with her. We spent an hour after breakfast looking for her ring in the bush.

The two girls and I also travelled up to Kinlochmoidart House, which is in the far north and extremely secluded, to do a gig for Alan. I was mesmerised by how the untouched lake near the house was so still; it looked like glass. A group of American families had rented the house for several days, partly to celebrate a member of the group's fortieth birthday. The three of us did a display of dances at various times during the evening. I went on to act the part of a servant maid who was with child by the Master of the House. I sat on a chaise-longue in my character clothes next to the table where they were eating, acting out the monologue for a short while before the guests realised I was acting and not just lounging around, chatting. I began sitting on the knees of all the men and blaming them for their advances. I recited another monologue about the ghost which haunted the House grounds. The name of the ghost and the script I wrote are long gone from my memory. Alan reminded me that our show had gone down a storm as we got a very long standing ovation.

After much persuasion from the girls, I ended up dancing in the show we did at the Moon Walk in Edinburgh in June 2006. I was the oldest girl in the group of dancers. My ankles were beginning to complain about all the bashing I had given them through many years of dancing. I had slowed down with the amount of dancing I was doing and was not overly keen initially to be involved in this show. The moon walk was a very big affair, where females were dressed in bras limbering up and having a party before their long walk to raise money for the Breast Cancer Charity. My favourite band Salsa Celtica was due to play after we had done our display and I was looking forward to jigging to their music. I had heard them play live a few times but had never performed in the same show as them.

As I was dancing the sword dance, my ankles seemed weak. I tamed down my dancing so as not to injure myself. It was later, when I was dancing another dance I experienced a burning sensation and heard a horrible pinging noise. My muscles had given up the ghost on my right leg. I found myself hopping on my left leg throwing my right leg about, enough to look as if I was dancing in a fashion until my part in the dance was over. I limped offstage, leaving the other dancer to finish her part of the dance. I couldn't stand on my right leg and found my left leg was weak. I was in agony and went back-stage to pack my legs with ice.

The members of the Salsa Celtica band were backstage at the same time so I managed to hobble around them to get a signature from them all. When they went on-stage to perform, I was raging about not being able to dance to their music. I could not walk properly for three months, never mind dance. Worse still, I was off my work for months and attended regular sessions of physiotherapy to help my leg heal. It really upset me to give up something I dearly loved, but I realised that keeping my regular job and providing for my family was more important than the fun I had dancing at events. Shortly after this gig, I sold all my dancing outfits, shoes and swords to make sure I would not be tempted to dance again. This was the last time I performed, dancing my Highland dancing, and it was to be the last time I worked with Alan.

Alan tells me that his attitude to life and how he was living it changed for the better after we had a deep chat following one of our gigs. He said: "You have had a certain influence on my life. It just goes to show you never know what effect one's words or actions have on other people." Alan has only just recently laid down his pipes for the last time. He can still be seen on his web page 'Stirling Highland Dancers' with all the dancers.

SINGLE LIFE

End of an Era

After trying a few weeks of marriage counselling, I eventually plucked up the courage and took my three children with me to a homeless refuge. There were other women and children staying in the safe house. The kitchen had the every-day items I needed to cook for my children until I was able to go shopping. Our bedrooms were separate but the lounge, kitchen and bathroom were communal. I was not permitted to tell anyone where I was to protect myself and the vulnerable women who lived in the house. There are houses like these all over Scotland, so when a woman is at risk of being found by who ever she is seeking refuge from, she is moved to another house in an unknown location. We stayed for a couple of nights, until I went to let my mum know where we were. She dragged us out of there to stay with her until we were given a place to stay.

We lived with my mum in a two-bedroom bungalow for eight months. It was taxing, as my children did not have space of their own to play. I phoned the social work department and asked if I could be given some help. The social work department could not help, because they claimed they had more desperate cases on their books. I did all the chores, but my mum was exhausted with the added stress of us constantly being around. I was offered a flat a few miles from my family and warned that if I did not accept it, the council would take me off the housing list. We stripped and decorated the flat as quickly and cheaply as we could before my children and I moved in.

In time, it transpired that my mum was very ill. She had attended quite a few doctor appointments but was assured the pain she experienced was caused by normal back problems. When the pain persisted, she was sent for further investigations. I sat outside the scanning room as I listened to the doctor telling me that my mum had Cancer. He discussed what the immediate plan of care was for her, but his words were fuzzy and distorted. My mind was still stuck on *my mum has Cancer*! She was whisked into theatre and had her kidney removed without having much time to think about it. Thankfully, the Cancer was caught in time, but they discovered that she was diabetic and required insulin, a risky condition for her remaining kidney. The hospital staff were amazed at how quickly my mum recovered from her operation. My dad told me he had been holding her hand through the whole ordeal and had sent her healing from Spirit.

I would like to say that with my mum getting better and us moving into a new home was the start of a fairytale story of a new life as a single parent with three children, but it wasn't. The apartments where we lived housed people with undesirable habits, such as the couple in the flat above us who were addicted to heroin. One man went up to complain about their noise but got stabbed in the stomach when an argument erupted. Late one night, the female from the flat above lay in a drug-induced sleep on the stairs beside her door. I was wakened by a policeman shouting at her to tell him where she lived. The constable was causing a commotion which threatened to wake my children so I opened the door, pointed to the woman's flat and coldly asked him to keep the noise down as I was up early for my work in the morning.

I did not permit my children to play around the flat due to all the dirty needles, filthy nappies and general rubbish lying around. Colin has red hair so was a prime target for being bullied at the less than desirable school he and Kevin had to go to. He used to run home from school away from the bullies just as Charlie had done all those years ago. I heard that Kevin was better at standing up for himself; the teachers told me he had taken a knife to school. I asked him about it and he denied it. I reprimanded him but thought that things must be bad for him to feel the need to protect himself with a knife. The last straw was when someone shot a pellet with a gun through my boys' bedroom window. It would have hit Kevin if he had been in bed on the top bunk of the bunk beds.

The marital home had been on the market for many months but was not selling. The estate agent informed me potential buyers were put off by the smell of stale smoke and the dampness caused by the bathroom shower. Eventually, it was deemed better for my children to move back into the marital home so they could go back to their old school and be with their old friends.

I tried keeping in-touch with my brothers-in-law and their families but eventually, I had to make a clean break away from them so we could all get on with our own lives. I had known them from the age of fifteen so they felt like my own family. I underestimated how much it would affect me to detach myself from them. I was especially fond of my ex-husband's nephew, who is also my godson. His mum was upset about me not being in his life, but I explained why many years later. There was no way I could try to make up for planning to be out of his life, but I wanted to give him something for his first communion day before I turned my back on him. I wrote a poem and had it printed on a little tee-shirt. I was surprised to learn he has kept it all these years.

Words For My Godson

A toy can get broken, clothes go out of fashion
and sweets melt and fade away.
What could I give my Godson on his first communion day?
Written words don't get broken, go out of fashion or fade away,
they can be forgotten but reread another day.
If there was only one piece of paper in the world left
on which I could write words to my godson,
this is what I would say:

When reaching for the stars,
don't let anyone grab you by the ankles and drag you down.
When finding your way through life,
hold your own map silently, close to your heart.
When singing your own song,
don't worry if you are out of tune with others,
for the sound of a free bird singing his own song
is the sweetest sound to be heard.

As long as you are singing from your heart
and your feet are tapping to your own beat,
you will have found the meaning of faith,
love and glory in all your endeavours.
Doing all this while keeping a smile in our pocket
will bring you revelation, joy and fulfilment.
This is the key which will open and spread peace in your life,
the kind of peace which will remain with you
forever being a faithful friend.

I wish you love, peace and protection in all that is to come.

Aunty Helen

Becoming a Midwife

I am only realising now how happy we were back in our home where we lived for many more years. I took over the mortgage of the house as by then I was training to be a midwife. Taking on a mortgage was a big risk for me as there was no guarantee I was going to be successful in qualifying as a midwife or obtain a job in this field. I knew it was a gamble, a huge commitment, so I studied extremely hard and tried my best to learn as much as I could on my placements. I finally made it through the three-year course and began sending out applications for a job.

It was difficult to get a job without experience and impossible to get experience without a job so I did what many newly qualified midwives did – I went to London. My mum was not over the moon about my plans to go there, but she agreed to look after my children while I went to a Hospital in London to work six twelve-hour shifts, followed by an early shift, then travelled home for four days off. I journeyed by bus, but if I managed to get cheap train tickets I took the train up and down. The first thing which struck me when I got nearer to London was the high volume of people compared to where I lived. The further south I went, the more I saw people from different countries. I found this interesting due to being from a small town of people who knew each other. The more people jammed into a train, the more they looked down or away. It was a form of detachment I was not used to. The feeling of being alone and so cut off from people made me feel disturbed; it made London seem like an unwelcoming and unsafe place.

When I reached the hospital I was to work in, I was given a key to a shared apartment in a high-rise block of flats. The single bedrooms were separate, with a lock on each door while the kitchen and toilets were communal. I liked the view I had out of my large window as I could see many miles of the English City. I took most of my basic needs with me but went shopping for some cooking utensils. I hopped onto a tube and went to Camden market to have a look around. I loved looking at all the homemade items on sale and felt at home amongst the people who were buying and selling items of a spiritual nature. I had been in London only a couple of weeks when I was asked out on a date by a young, good-looking man who was from Africa. I did not see any point in perusing a relationship with him or any other man as I was there to work and gain experience and had no intention of remaining there.

My working day started with taking my turn to get into the shower and prepare some porridge, which at times was the only food I got till I finished my daily shift. I was intrigued by my flat-mate who showered wearing flip-flops. I wondered if I should be concerned about cross-infection in the flat. When I made my way over to the large hospital, the girls in the labour ward restored my faith in the people of London as they were so welcoming. I became interested in all the different backgrounds the girls had and was grateful for all the different ways of working in midwifery they taught me. One kind ward sister from Jamaica sat me down and advised me that the work in London was so hard and fast – I had to give what I could to the women, but I also had to hold a little bit back for myself. She said the fast pace of the ward could wear me down very quickly. I had admiration for her as she did not know me but took the time to consider my health and wellbeing. I came to realise that there are many lovely people who are like hidden gems amongst the huge population jungle of London. I was fortunate to be young with oodles of energy, as the pace was indeed phenomenal and the workload back-breaking most days. Even though we were busy, the girls took time to have a quick chat and a bit of a laugh throughout the day. Occasionally, at the end of a shift, we would all trundle to the local pub for a quick debriefing and reflecting session.

A few times, I took a couple of hours for myself before travelling home at the end of my block of shifts. I travelled to the shops to see what everyone was raving about. Harrods and many other shops like it were shops I would look in but not purchase anything from. I found many items in designer shops with the price ticket hidden; when I twisted the ticket around I thought: *How much*?? In one shop, I found a pair of jeans full of designer holes priced at three hundred pounds. I was on a different planet to the one I was used to. Hamleys Toy shop is one store I enjoyed browsing around. I was over the moon to be able to purchase one of the last Harry Potter Lego train sets for my boys who were fanatics. I managed to obtain it just hours before it was televised on TV – there were only eight sets left in UK which could be bought before Christmas, and they were being sold at Hamleys in London.

It was heartbreaking to see people on the streets. Some of them looked genuinely down in their luck, but many were professional beggars who were there to con kind-hearted people out of their money. It was hard to know the difference between the people who really needed help and those who didn't. One guy was convincing enough to scam money out of me at a bus station when I first arrived there. It was only a few pounds, but it provided me with a lifetime lesson not to be so gullible in such a big city. It was after this experience I learnt there are professional rings of males and females who sit in places such as bus or train stations and at main tourist attraction areas to give their fabricated hard-luck stories in order for people to give them money out of pity.

One young girl posed as a student and sat beside a man who looked a bit odd and less able than most. She began her show of tears in order for the guy to notice her so she could begin her story to try and get money from him. I could see he was aware of what she was up to and completely ignored her. I was intrigued by how she went about conning people so watched her trying her best to get his attention. I couldn't stop myself laughing at her when she tried a bit harder, but to no avail. In response to me staring and laughing, she got up and moved to the far side of the bus station to wait and start again with another victim.

I got a bit lost one time while I was out and about so asked a woman where the nearest station was. She directed me in her foreign accent, then tried to give me a story about how her boyfriend had kicked her out without giving her money. Every time I gave her possible answers to her fabricated problems, she would reply with another hardluck line. I walked faster than her towards the tube station so I could make my way home to my family and shouted back at her: "You should go to the embassy, they will sort you out!" I was a single parent with three children at home. I wondered what made these people think I had money to give them. Nowadays, people are scammed out of money online and by bogus phone calls from these kinds of people.

I only worked in London travelling up and down for three months as I intended to start studying for my Honours degree in midwifery in the following three months, but I still had a mortgage to pay. I managed to get three months of full-time work at Prudential in Stirling. At that time, it was known as 'The Scottish Amicable.' I enjoyed working as a Keyer in the Data department, keying information into data bases with great speed and accuracy. I had been doing this temporary job on and off before my midwifery training so knew the staff well. When all the data input was complete each day, I was moved to help in other departments such as the filing and imaging department, where all the mail was scanned and filed onto computers.

When this temporary job ended, I began work at Dunblane golf club, where I worked in the kitchen and served meals to the members. I got on really well with the couple who were both chefs and the other staff, except for one guy. He was a trainee chef and thought he was above us all. His behaviour was abysmal when the bosses were out of the building. He took things off the trays I had arranged with salt and sauce sachets to take meals downstairs to the customers. One day, the male boss ticked me off for not putting an item on the tray, an item this boy had taken off when I was otherwise occupied. I did not divulge what the boy was doing. I resorted to leaving that job as soon as I could. The wages had been exceptionally good when I worked in London, so I decided I would go back to work there after I completed the first block of modules for my studies. The bosses of the golf club were shocked to learn that I was a qualified midwife. I omitted the qualification from my CV as I did not want to appear over-qualified for their job. They were disappointed I was leaving and said: "You are deserting a sinking ship."

Natalie was only five years old, so she was the most affected when I decided to leave her again. The sight of her crying at the station when I left on the train still lies heavy in my mind. Her distress pulled at my heart, but I had no choice but to try and get more experience in midwifery and pay all my bills. This three-months trip away was not as pleasurable as the previous one. The fire alarms in the nurse's accommodation where I slept kept activating and car alarms around the hospital sounded out through a lot of the nights. Added to the broken sleep, the work in the labour ward seemed even more taxing. As before, we hardly got a break to eat through the twelve-to-fourteenhour shifts. Members of the Jewish community came into the labour ward to hand in dry food. Some of their food kept us going.

A few nights before I was due to finish my second block of working there, I went to a shop near the hospital. A bag of shopping cost three times as much as it did at home, but I needed provisions for the rest of the week and for the long journey home. I had a bag of shopping in each hand and earphones on my ears listening to music from my walkman as I walked in the darkness. I noticed an overly thin black male who appeared to bounce as he walked up and down the pavement outside a pub at the top of the street. I began walking down the hill towards the hospital and was about to make my way down a secluded pathway which had some bushes at the bottom of the hill on my right. I got an ache in my stomach, warning me something was not right with this man, who was by then following me. I slowed my pace and wondered what to do. A voice instructed me to "stop, turn around and look him straight in the eye." I did as this voice said and looked at the strange man. I looked deeply into his eyes, then studied his bandana and skimpy clothing for a few seconds before he unexpectedly turned around and began bouncing back up the hill. I had no fear while I was silently confronting him but realised the seriousness of the situation when I noticed something silver glinting in his left hand under the street lamp as he passed it. I made the conscious effort to walk the long way around the hospital to the staff accommodation block rather than take the shorter secluded pathway. This man must have been known to the police, because special undercover police men urgently wanted to talk to me about him. There were so many lovely people in London who I worked and socialised with, but due to this experience I have not had the urge to work there again.

My brother Charlie had a problem with some of the nerves of his face so when he had surgery at a hospital about an hour away, I went to visit him. I got a homely feeling with this hospital and somehow just knew it would be where I would work. My mum drove my car to take me to a job interview, because I had just finished a block of shifts in London and was extremely tired. We were jumping up and down

I want to be happy and bright,
wear a smile not a frown.
I'll be okay, I'll be fine
when you turn your back
for one last time.

So, let go of my hand
is the message I send.
I'm getting on with life
but missing a friend.

Salsa Escapades

I began filling my single life with a different kind of social life. I met my best friend Lorna when my eldest son, Kevin, was seven years old and went to the Boys Brigade in Bannockburn. When Lorna was picking her son up from the group, we began chatting. She had lived in Germany as a daughter of a soldier and spoke fluent German so we clicked straight away. We spent a lot of time together as she was also separated from her husband. We started a lifelong friendship and began going to salsa classes in a hall near the Wallace Monument in Stirling. I found it refreshing to mix with people to dance without bothering about the dating scene. The salsa world is a close-knit group, like a family or a community containing people of many nationalities. Everyone is welcome from all walks of life to meet up and just dance. A man can approach a woman to ask her for a dance and vice versa and they can be reassured that dancing is all it is about. Some people come to UK on holiday and don't speak English, but salsa moves are generally universal in all countries.

People who love to dance don't drink much alcohol as it is very hard for a man to make dance signals for a woman to understand if he is drunk. Women would not be able to pick up on the man's hand signals if they were drunk either so both parties could be badly hurt. If we see someone who is drunk at a salsa party or event, it is usually someone who is a non-dancer, a beginner who has yet to realise that drink and salsa dancing don't mix, or a dancer who has had a bad day or has popped in after a night out somewhere else. Everyone can party without fear of there being any trouble at salsa events. At pubs and night clubs, a man might make a move on a drunken woman for obvious reasons. At salsa events, men run fearing they could be injured by them.

I am not saying dating did not go on amongst salsa dancers; it most certainly did. Many mixed or same-sex couples met at salsa classes or dancing events and are still together today. I dated one guy in the Stirling group but in the end, he was more interested in a super-slim girl who suffered from anorexia. She kept him hanging on as she already had a boyfriend but wanted a regular dance partner. Lorna had been his platonic dance partner for some time but was dropped like a hot brick. We could see what this girl was doing, but it was none of our business. My friendship with this man was never the same, because dating him overstepped the boundaries. Lorna and I had many offers but turned most of them down; we mainly went to salsa events for the dancing.

There was a terminology in the salsa world called 'Salsa goggles.' This phrase meant pretty young girls would date male salsa dancers, because they could move regardless of their looks. One guy who was not attractive ended up marrying a pretty, tall girl who was a fashion model. The same guy taught a class I went to. He regularly had us all in a circle doing a kind of dance many couples danced together. He was showing the group a new Rhoada move while he danced with me, but he somehow ended up with his hand under my skirt and up my lady bits. Instinctively, I swung around and slapped him across his face. Everyone knew what he had done so were falling about the place, laughing. I had to apologise for my involuntary reaction, but I don't remember him apologising for what he had done.

If a hall was jumping with lots of dancers, it became necessary for women to grab men before a song began, otherwise those who had been slow in picking a man to dance to a favourite track would remain standing or left to mark the beat with some solitary footwork. I began trying to dance with very experienced dancers to push myself to learn more moves than the classes were teaching me. I had good rhythm and found it hard to dance with men who danced off-beat. I would check out their movements and their dancing feet before I danced with them, but there were exceptions when good friends were danced with out of respect, regardless of their ability. One time in the early days when I was very much a beginner, one dancer took my fancy to dance with so I ran to him and asked for a dance. He stopped and walked off half-way through the dance as he realised I didn't know many of his moves. This was considered very rude in the salsa world, but he did it all the same. A good lead can make any level of dancer move well. Later, when I was an experienced dancer, I clocked him in a salsa bar in Glasgow and asked him to dance again. Before the music began, I told him he had been rude and chucked me half-way through a dance. He smiled and said: "So, you are here to kick my butt now?" I nodded my head and gave him a wicked grin. We danced to a fast track while I gave him a run for his money. After the dance he laughed: "Okay, I think you kicked my butt."

When I was still fairly new on the scene, I had all the Stirling group of dancers in stitches when we were at a big event in Edinburgh. I did my usual and ran up to a guy to ask for a dance before the next music track started. His feet didn't move much, but he had good rhythm. I had watched him twirl his female dance partners around while he conserved his energy, marking the beat with his feet and now and then came out with some smart footwork. This kind of dancing interested me so I waited with excitement for the music to start. When I realised a super-fast track was starting, an involuntary swear word came from my mouth. He noticed my friends laughing at my face of shock. We all knew it was going to be a hard dance for me to keep up with. He had me burling and twirling and jigging this way and that way at a super-fast speed. My friends were on the floor with laughter by the time the track finished.

A group of us car-shared, travelling to many salsa events all over Scotland. The music was mostly played on a deck, but occasionally we had the pleasure of dancing to live salsa bands. Lorna was more into the music than I was. She took great interest in the lead singer of the Salsa Celtica band, getting all excited when he was singing. We were in Glasgow at the Classic Grand when she kept shouting: "There he is!" I couldn't see what all the fuss was about, but I looked anyway for all I could see without my long-distance glasses. Lorna now has this lovely man as her partner.

For me, everything was about the dancing, until I was dancing in a club and as usual the place was packed. The night was in full swing when I noticed a guy who took my interest. He couldn't dance for peanuts so was obviously there for the social life rather than to perfect his dance moves. I started talking to him and before long, we began dating. He would stay over at my house and I would sometimes stay over at his flat. We were what I considered to be boyfriend and girlfriend. He was from Turkey but was about to obtain a British passport as he had been working in Scotland for nearly ten years. He was more into the British way of living than the Turkish way of life. I fell for him deeply, but my mum did not take to him. As usual, though, she let me do my own thing. My brother Charlie had been a driving instructor for many years so taught my boyfriend to drive. I took him out in my car many times to practise, until I realised he always thought he was right when he clearly was in the wrong. Natalie spent a lot of time with my boyfriend and me. She scrunched a piece of paper while he was driving, then showed him the shrivelled paper: "Look what you are doing to me!" She didn't think highly of his driving either, so I drove the car from then on when she was with us. Charlie fitted a new kitchen for him and I helped him renovate his flat. We seemed to be getting on like a house on fire and then, one

Christmas, he went home to Turkey for the first time in over a year since I had been dating him.

After another year of dating, I sensed that he would not be my boyfriend for much longer. It seemed as if someone was giving me a pre-warning. I looked up into the air and pleaded with Spirit: "Please, don't take my man away from me!" The spirit who was with me advised me to go to his spare-room and look in a satchel which was concealed behind a bedroom unit. I had no idea what I was going to find in the bag so I sat down and opened it slowly. I took a deep breath as I knew it was not going to be good news. I found a picture of my boyfriend holding hands with a young girl wearing wedding clothes. Then a voice asked me to look at other pictures so I scanned through photos on his camera. The same girl was in all the pictures but worst of all, so was the date they were taken. I drove to his work and asked to see him immediately. We sat in my car while he told me that he had gone home to get married to his eighteen-year-old cousin, nineteen years younger than him. He said the marriage had been arranged for many years, but he thought he had made a mistake going through with it. He told me he would finish his relationship with her as he wanted to stay in Britain with me.

During our courtship, he had bought phone cards and phoned home to Turkey many times while I sat beside him, but I did not realise he had been talking to his wife. I learnt a little Turkish and hired a Turkish interpreter; I phoned his family to tell them all about me. This is how I found out that he was supposed to have got married much sooner and how they had realised that I was the reason he had delayed it. Through this phone call, I was able to confirm that he had gone home and got married. I asked him why he had continued our relationship for more than a year after his wedding. He replied: "It is my right to have four women!" In response, I thought: *it is my right to shut the door behind me*. I had been lied to for two years. At the beginning when we met, I had asked him if I was someone he would date until he had an arranged marriage. He never answered the question – so, omitting to answer the question was as much a lie as a lie is; more fool me.

When I collected my children and got home, I crouched on the stairs of my home. I felt as if someone had blown a hole through my heart. I cried silent tears into a pillow so my children would not hear me. I asked Spirit to take some of the pain away as it was all too much. I had given into love and had my heart pulled out in the process once more. Also, my Nana Hamilton had died so I hid myself away in my room most nights when my children were in bed. I lit some candles and began a reading marathon, reading books about the afterlife and alternative therapies.

When I went to the Spiritualist Church, I got a reading from a psychic woman in which my Nana and Papa Hamilton came through with a message for me. They told me to put the new clothes on which hung in my wardrobe with labels still attached and get back out dancing, or they would take away the staff and the green healing light they were shining to show me the way. This was typical of my Nana Hamilton. When I was sad she would raise my chin, smile and say: "Chin up!" I have every confidence that it was her who helped me find out what my Turkish man had been up to, because we had had a conversation about his behaviour before she died. She said: "All will come out in the wash."

The reasons for my Nana being tired and feeling ill also came out in the wash. My mum and I had noticed that she was spending an unnatural amount of time in the toilet and that she was becoming unexplainably tired on our shopping sprees. My mum and I took her to a doctor to find out what was going on. Doctors hold the key of the locked door to the room of further investigation and appropriate treatment, but my Nana had let her symptoms get beyond help before we were able to encourage her to have investigations. I am guessing she did this because she told us she did not want to get old. The doctor sat calmly and told her she had Cancer. He believed that she had known for some time, and he gave her an approximation of six months to live.

She received intensive radiotherapy treatment which she felt didn't help her; it made her more ill. My mum hoped to care for my Nana in her own home, but she could not continue without help. It was too much for my mum to watch her in such pain. A few days before we realised my Nana was going to die, she was in hospital. She said she felt well and did not understand why she was in hospital. She never came home; she was placed into a corner room of the receiving ward, because they realised she was on the way to the afterlife rather than on the way out to another ward. My mum, her sister and brother sat with my Nana day and night. I sat with her for a period of time to allow everyone to go home and get showered and eat.

My Nana had smoked all her life so it was no surprise to learn that she had lung cancer, amongst other things. People of her generation had no idea what cigarettes could do to the body. I understood it was the trend to smoke in her day and she was unable to stop the habit. I watched her struggle to catch a breath and thought: *if people knew the horrible death of lung cancer which could be before them, they might think twice about smoking*. I often wondered whether my Nana did not seek medical help earlier because she may have wanted to join her husband in the afterlife. She talked to him as if he was sitting in the room. She called out, asking him to help her so I sent out a thought: *how long*? I was given the number three. Three days later

I was at home, completely bogged down with the 'flu, too ill to sit with her, when I smelt her familiar smell and sensed her visiting me in my bedroom. My mum and Bert came to my door to tell me that she was gone. I opened the door and before they had time to tell me, I said: "I know."

I did not know how to deal with the loss of my Nana and my Turkish man. I cried my eyes out night after night, wondering what life was all about. During this time, I thought living meant nothing but pain. My friend Lorna was learning to be a DJ at salsa events so it was she who dragged me back out to dance. I continued to dance at places where I knew the Turkish man would not be, especially since his wife had been forced by her family to move over to Britain to be with him.

I mentally visualised him out of my mind and out of my life. I began by beaming a virtual laser clockwise all around my body to cut away the energy cords which linked us. Using the laser, I gently healed the areas where the cords had been attached, before I sent the cords back to him. I finished separating our energy by imagining we were both on an island floating on water. I separated us by cutting the island in two. I pushed him on his half of the island, further away from me every day. I then added a tall brick wall between us so I could not reach him and he could not reach me mentally or in a spiritual sense. Eventually, I forgot all about him and what he had done.

Visualisations for linking to or detaching people from our lives are personal. It is the intent rather than the specific visualisation which makes it effective. It must be done with love, because sending out negative energy rebounds back to us more than we will ever understand. The saying 'Like attracts like' emphasises the attraction or rebounding of negative and positive molecules of magnetic energy. When I wish to protect myself from negative vibrations, I imagine myself in the centre of a circle of tall mirrors facing outwards, away from me. The mirrors reflect the negative energy back to its source. This visualisation must always finish with us sending out thoughts of love to the source of the offending vibrations.

After ending my relationship with the Turkish man, I did not want to date again for over four years. I wondered what there was to gain from the emotional pain of being in a relationship. I am realising now that my spiritual plan was to experience as many emotions as opposed to my past life, where I learned about detachment of emotions. I had enough of the pain of love and attraction. I remembered my prayer years ago, asking for more experiences in life so looked up into the air: *Okay guys up there, I have had enough of this. I just want to live a nice easy life now. Thanks*!

Learning the Ropes

It is ironic – the happiest time of my life and most stressfree period was when no men were anywhere near me. I was working as a midwife and was enjoying having fun with my children. We loved having movie nights at weekends. I look back on these happy times and really miss my boys and Natalie being snuggled in with our carpet picnics while watching movies on the television.

When my children were doing their own thing, I started to fill some of my spare time by attending alternative therapy courses. My work encouraged the use of aromatherapy oils in the maternity suite so I wanted to be qualified to use them, too. I studied a Diploma course in Aromatherapy and Massage at Cardonald College in Glasgow. It was there I met my good friend Janet. When we were training, we were supposed to give each other massages and swap partners every week. We preferred to stay with each other, giving and receiving a massage. It worked for us as we were able to give and receive honest feedback of all our sessions. This helped us to improve our techniques. When we finished the year-long course, we enrolled for another course together, then another, and another. We attained many Diplomas in alternative therapies and became great friends. I travelled to her home in Dumbarton and she came to my house to continue our massage therapy treatments and have a good chat. I realised my life was starting to take a new direction, involving more of my spiritual side.

As my confidence grew, I gave my family and friends alternative therapy and healing sessions at home. They told their friends and families about my sessions so by word of mouth I ended up with quite a few people coming for treatments or just for relaxation. I charged a minimum fee for the oils and my time and rarely charged for psychic healings as it cost nothing to do them. Sometimes, I would only charge the cost of the fuel when people asked me to go to their house to help them. One woman told me she had been trying to have a baby for a long time and was advised that alternative therapies could help her. I couldn't promise her anything but worked on the points in her body I knew would increase her fertility and finished with a healing session. She phoned me not too long after her treatment to tell me that she was pregnant. My colleague Gillian asked me to give her a foot massage during a slack period at work. She then told me a couple of weeks later she was pregnant and blamed me for it.

My client list grew until one guy came for a massage while my children were upstairs watching television. He got undressed and was lying naked under his towel. I felt uneasy giving him a massage without his underwear on. I am sure it would have been a different story if I was in a massage parlour with other adults around. When I went back into the room with the oils for the massage he was lying face up showing all. I was single and had not seen equipment like his for a long time so it would have been great to think about it, but what he was doing was sleazy. I should have told him to get dressed and get out, but I gave him the benefit of the doubt. I gave him the hour massage he came for, then asked for feedback. He picked up the towel covering himself and said he would have preferred the massage without the towel. A couple of weeks later, he tried to book another session, but I told him I didn't massage men any more. Following this experience, I only gave massage treatments to men I knew, or men of women I knew. I discovered that there was someone in my area who gave extras with their massage treatments but it certainly was not me.

I got a phone call from a man who asked if I would do a naturist massage for him and his wife. At first, I thought it was a wind-up and then in my limited thinking I thought he wanted a massage for some sort of sexual pleasure. I asked him to explain what he wanted. He said he wanted him and his wife to be naked while I gave them both a massage. I replied: "I don't get paid enough for that, thank you." One of my friends asked me if the couple expected me to be naked, too. I told her that I did not continue with the conversation long enough to find out.

When I think of that phone call I linked it with an experience I had recently. I sat in a private waiting room with a few people, dressed as they were, in a hospital gown. I was intrigued at how their energy appeared different when they were stripped of their belongings and their social status. We all gave the appearance of equal beings, free from the weight of possessions and responsibility while waiting to have the same hospital treatment. I wondered if this is what it feels like to be a nudist. I get upset when people try to associate sleaze with massage treatments and wonder if people get annoyed when their nudity is viewed as sleaze. Each to their own, but there will always be a selected few who bring disrepute into massage and nudity. Many people look to obtain a level of euphoria from physical pleasure but may be unaware they can reach a kind of euphoria by working on their spiritual energy.

Just Different

When you are sensitive to spiritual energy, you view life very differently to those who are closed down from their spiritual self. I was in my car waiting with my mum, the reason for us being in the car escapes me, but the conversation sticks in my mind. We were reminiscing about our past, and my mum talked about my two brothers and me fondly. When finished describing my brothers and how well they have done in their lives, she turned away to think for a minute about me. She finally settled on the statement of "Well, you're just different," like the word 'different' is used for something you can't explain. This is a statement some mediums say is used for people who are sensitive to spiritual energy. If someone starts a sentence with 'You are different,' the likelihood is that you are different. I am only different in my mum's eyes, because we have differing views on the existence of an afterlife and the benefits of healing energy, even though she has benefited from numerous healing sessions from me. It took her to pay someone else to give her a Reiki healing before she realised I could do just the same for her. It appears that some treatments are considered more effective if there is a charge for the service.

My earliest memory of having a sense of something out of the ordinary was when I was around 6 years old, sitting on my Nana and Papa Hamilton's kitchen window ledge. I was looking out of the window, day-dreaming for some time when a huge tree took my interest. I knew the tree would somehow feature in my future. I could feel something would be beside the tree, but didn't know what. I was surprised a random thing like a tree could grab my attention for so long. I forgot all about this incident until many years later, when my mum showed me the new house she had bought. It was a bungalow which was situated next to the tree.

Young children often have a sixth sense, but this awareness usually lessens when they are distracted by being emerged into every-day life such as going to school. My Papa Nicol tested me once during a trip to the park with my younger cousin. I had no idea why he was testing either my psychic or telepathic ability. It took many years for me to find out that his mother, my Great-Gran, regularly read people's tealeaves and could predict their future. He said I had her eyes and was like her. I had no idea what he was talking about at the time.

I was known as a dreamer when I was a child. I don't remember being pushed or helped to fulfil my full potential while at school by the teachers or by my family. My dad said: "Just do your best" and "A job is not worth doing if you are not going to do it right." I just winged it at school and didn't try my best. There were so many other interesting things to day-dream about. It was not until after my dad came forward during a reading I had with a psychic medium that he expressed his surprise at how busy my mind was. He was able to hear my thoughts so realised my dreamy nature was actually me taking time to look at things and think a great deal about them from all different angles.

I find it fascinating how people can share an experience but have differing opinions on them. My Nana Hamilton was walking with me on one of our shopping trips towards the town when she suddenly turned to me and said: "What a mess!" She was pointing at apple-blossom flowers covering the street, road and people's gardens. Seconds before her outburst, I had looked at all the blossom and thought: *how wonderful, the blanket of pink flowers covered the place as if they were spreading love everywhere.*

What we experience and learn through life can affect how we view the world around us. We live in a world with verbal and non-verbal clues and symbolic meanings which we can use to assist us in making sense of everything. A person who lives in an expensive house at the top of a large hill could be viewed as just that, a lucky so and so. Another angle would be to view that person as someone who has a hard up-hill struggle to keep what they have or can be a person who needs to feel regal or safe on top of a hill like a king in a castle on high ground.

I was easily distracted when things out of the ordinary happened. I got a hiding from my aunt when she left my two-year-old cousin under my care for a short time when I was eleven years old. It was not unusual for me to look after my two cousins, but this time I was enthralled by their next-door neighbour's children who were playing with a Ouija board in their shed. We were all engrossed in the game, watching the glass move from side to side, wondering if someone was pushing it. My young cousin was in the shed with us but must have sneaked out and wandered off. It took some time for us all to find him.

I had the experience of playing with a Ouija board a few times. At Fiona's house, we asked the unknown source to perform validation tricks. We witnessed pieces of paper folding on top of each other, a candle flame going down to a tiny flicker and returning to a full-powered blaze and noises when we asked for them. We played the Ouija board in a caravan my Papa Hamilton had stored in our driveway. When my mum came into the caravan to see what we were up to, we chucked everything under the table and pretended to be working on our school project. I realise now how lame that story was. Later that night, I did not know what to do with the glass so I hid it under my bed. During the night, my bed lifted up into the air and banged down hard. I jumped out of bed and ran to sit in my mum's room. My mum got angry telling me how dangerous it was playing the Ouija board game as it has unknown forces associated with it. The next day, I took the glass and washed it out with water and smashed it into pieces on the ground. I was told this ritual would get rid of unwanted spirits, but even to this day I am not sure how accurate this advice is. I guess playing the game was a bid to find out more about the spirit world, albeit in the wrong way.

My Great-Gran died when I was a teenager. She was the spirit who came forward many times to give me advice when I went to have psychic readings from mediums. Among the usual every-day advice I was given, she told me people are like puppets and those in the afterlife hold the strings. We live our lives with free will, but they give us nudges and suggestions and help us when we need assistance. They guide us on our pre-agreed pathways of life in order for us to feel emotions, learn lessons and evolve. So why don't we all hear 'them upstairs' and why do we not get all the answers we need? One way to rationalise this would be to say: what would be the point of living and experiencing life's gifts if we already had the answers? Spirit advised me to stop dreaming of winning money as this was not what life was about. If we are not the chosen lottery winner it may be because we would not take a particular job or choose a path which could lead us to our preferred goal if we had wads of money.

I didn't think too much about the messages from my Great-Gran at the time as I was in the throws of human life. I was more surprised when at another reading she asked if I could let her go. I had no idea what this meant. I did not feel I was holding onto her, and anyway, where was she going? I had limited knowledge of the afterlife at this time and no-one in my immediate family seemed remotely interested in the subject. This reading made me think that there was more to being here on earth and in the afterlife than it appeared, so I began reading more books about spirituality and the afterlife. It was the knowledge of there being an afterlife which got me through the thought of having to change my life drastically. My life as I knew it was about to change when I was twenty-eight years old. I knew my marriage was coming to an end, but I was in turmoil. My husband was a good father so I could not understand why something so wrong for my children could be so right for me.

I began visiting the spiritual church as I needed a crutch to lean on. Being around like-minded people heightened my psychic ability. It helped me realise what was in my heart was right and true for a greater good. I was given support and reassurance and an insight into what I already knew I needed to do. They helped me through my divorce by giving me many healing sessions. The loss of my marriage made me question my beliefs and the kind of life I lived. Loss can come in many guises; it does not necessary mean we are losing a loved one from our life or from our world. We may have to accept change when we experience loss of our state of health or possessions we have had. Some people are devastated at the thought of not being able to have something or someone they would dearly like in their lives and that is a kind of loss.

It is not something I advertise, but I have been what is called a healer for many years and have helped quite a few people through the years. I understand proof is required in order to give yourself the title of being a healer and to be able to promote the ability of being able to heal someone. Those who give healings are just a catalyst as healing comes within. Healers act as part of a circuit board which is connected to a higher vibration or energy source. The receiver is helped to plug into the circuit board to boost and alter their own energy system. The healer accesses this electrical current in order to boost the receiver's healing ability if it is the receiver's higher wish to be healed. It is a practice which has been used for many years and is something some mediums say is used on the other side, especially when returning home after a physical life on Earth. We have all used the powerful, colourful crystal healing chambers in the spirit world at one time or another. I am grateful for all the teachings I received from the kind members of the Spiritual Church. They taught me about a deeper meaning to life and about what happens to us after we die. I was invited into a development circle which was very enlightening. We used telepathy and psychic skills to read each other. I was taught techniques which helped heighten my vibrations when working with Spirit. I enjoyed games involving guessing what was hidden in boxes or behind screens. I seem to have a talent reading people by looking at their photos, I can sense many things about a person from their photograph. I was intrigued to learn that when the sclera of a subject is dull and lifeless in a photo it can mean they are no longer living. I used colour ribbons to read people. I learned colours have different vibrations and are associated with many things in life. Feeling the vibrations of the coloured ribbons inspired me to study colour-healing therapies more.

Some therapists use colour lights to achieve a particular effect. Other people act as a life coach and advise their clients to incorporate certain colours in their clothing and homes. I realise we each choose the colour of our clothes and items around us in relation to how we feel each day. People in establishments use colours to benefit the clients who use their services and to aid the success of their business. Some restaurants decorate their establishments in the colour red to increase people's speed in which they digest food to ensue customers eat faster. It is thought that the amount of people who can dine each day increases as a result. Some establishments use blue in their décor to reduce blood pressure or injections of purple or pink for general healing. Too much of one colour in our lives can have a detrimental effect on us. Colours are linked to each of our chakras so our medical conditions are linked to a particular chakra and colour. We use colours productively in alternative therapies such as crystal or flower therapy. Occasionally, I see colours associated with the receiver's illness or disease when I give healing sessions.

I was guided on how to open up before each healing session and how to close down safely. This involved learning how to ground and protect myself. We need to ground ourselves before working with energy as the change in our vibrations can make us feel unsteady and out of balance. It is important to protect ourselves when we open up and raise our vibrations when linking with energy sources or Spirit as there are less- desirable spirits who can come near us. We are the controller so we can demand that these souls leave us or we can close ourselves down and ask Spirit to help remove them while visualising extra protection around us.

Protection visualisations are helpful during our daily life, because the people around us can unwittingly damage or suck our energy away. Most people can recall situations when their energy has been boosted or drained when around certain people, animals or things. Some spiritually-minded people believe this is one of the reasons people gain weight when living and working in stressful situations or with dependent people. We subconsciously make ourselves bigger and heavier to help ground and protect ourselves from these energy vampires.

My healing session begins with asking for healing from the light, from the higher source and all that is good. I ask Spirit to come forward to give the receiver a healing if it is to be given at that time. I then ground myself and the receiver. I imagine my feet are heavy in my shoes, touching the ground underneath me. I ask the receiver to put their feet flat on the floor if they are sitting or to relax into the therapy bed if they are lying down. I then imagine us both having three ropes or tree roots. One is tied around the left ankle, one around the right ankle and one around the tail bone. The roots reach down to the core of the Earth and tie tightly around it.

I then ask Spirit for protection for myself and the receiver. I encase myself in a protective bubble by drawing a virtual circular protective layer around me and a separate one around the receiver. This is done by visualising a white or golden light beaming from the crown of the head and around the body clockwise, until the circle is sealed. On occasions, I use my dolphin crystal wand to do this. In challenging situations, I add the visualisation of putting on a light silky cloak of protection. The impermeable garment covers me from head to foot and has buttons or a zip I use to keep it closed tight until the session is complete. The colour of the cloak is personal to each healer. I use purple for spiritual progression.

I ask the receiver to take three deep breaths while I breathe with them to link with their energy. I put my hands on or just above the receiver's shoulders or around their head to wait for Spirit to connect with me and begin. I usually give healings without touching the receiver, but this is mostly due to it being the way my spirit guides wish me to work. I am directed to the parts of the receiver's body which needs healed by Spirit giving me verbal or visual directions and by their vibrations in my hands as I scan the receiver's body. I can hold a person's hand and the healing can be sent to where it is needed. I can work through the Reiki sequence if the receiver wishes a Reiki healing, but I have found directed healing is quicker and just as effective. I finish every healing session by thanking Spirit for their help. I then remove the virtual protection and rope or tree bonds, once I have closed the energy link down. I always inform the receiver what messages Spirit wants to relay or explain what I have felt during the session. Sometimes, what I impart doesn't make sense to me but makes sense to the receiver.

When I was training, I was more attracted to giving psychic healings than giving readings. My upbringing and life experiences have made me a blunt, truthful person so I found it difficult knowing what information to give to the receiver and what to hold back. More intensive training would be required to learn this diplomatic skill. Once, I witnessed a young girl hesitantly admitting she had a psychological problem in-front of a few hundred people to verify the message the medium was about to pass on was for her. The audience was amazed at the medium's accuracy, but I am sure the girl was mortified and withdrew and shut her energies down from the medium and all the other people in the room. In the end, there was no message for this girl, only embarrassment. The members of the Spiritual Church get around hurting people by asking the receiver if they can take a description or message rather than have the receiver divulge validation details. There can be times when there are so many loved ones trying to get through to the living at one sitting. Spirit can somehow send one message which can help more than one person at the same time. Great responsibility comes from being a psychic medium, as care is required to translate Spirit's messages correctly and sensitively. Two of my medium friends have been threatened by families of the sitters they gave readings to, because the messages imparted upset one or more parties. Even the most diplomatic tuned-in medium who translates Spirit's messages accurately could experience a disillusioned sitter or one who completely misinterprets what is said. Messages which are said to come from Spirit can have unforeseen consequences, so I guess this may be why British mediums legally have to state that their readings are for entertainment only.

The first healing session I had myself was electrifying. It was as if someone had plugged my finger into a socket and gave me the most pleasant current through my body. It was relaxing, yet invigorating at the same time. I came out of a relaxed state when the leader of the group finished her healing session on me. I turned to face her and said: "Wow, that was better than sex!" She laughed and replied: "I will take your word for it." Being a member of the church and giving healings regularly took great commitment, but it was enjoyable.

I did not advertise my abilities at home or work, but if people around me had a problem I would offer to help them. A friend and colleague called Sharon had a painful jaw; it clicked and moved unnaturally. She was due to go into hospital for an operation to fix the problem. I gave her a fifteen-minute healing which I could feel was very intense. The following week, she told me she did not need the operation any more as her jaw was healed. My colleague Neera banged her knee on a heavy suitcase. The pain disappeared after I gave her a quick healing during a break at work. Another colleague had a sore back when I was working in a special-care baby unit, so I gave her a quick zap of psychic healing. She was over the moon – her back was better; but later that day we laughed, because she tripped over an incubator and put it out again.

I seem to have an ability to help people with sore backs. My mother in-law was desperate to play an important grass-bowling game, but she could hardly stand, never mind play bowls. I was able to heal her back so she was able to play her game and win it. I gave her healings on her back a few times after that and each time it worked. When I was at her bowling club in Airdrie, some of her friends set up a chair in the kitchen and lined up for me to give them all a short healing session. My mother-in-law joked: "Should you be healing the opposition team members?"

One woman came to my house to have a massage and healing session as a 'thank you' for her husband repairing brick work in my house. She phoned me two days later, asking me what I had done to hurt her back. This elderly woman was seen jigging on the dance-floor of her bowling club a few hours after my session. I phoned my massage tutor for advice. She agreed with me – there was nothing in the massage treatment which could have hurt her. Psychic healing can cause tears to flow as it can help the receiver to express pent-up emotions, but it never causes damage. I gave the woman another healing out of courtesy, but this experience taught me a great deal about the importance of the legalities regarding alternative therapies, regardless of whether money changes hands or not.

I began getting more images and messages during my healing sessions. My brother David was off sick from his work when I was up north visiting my family. I pulled a chair into the kitchen and gave him a healing. I got an image of him so was able to readvise him of how he could change his posture and the mode in which he was doing a particular repetitive task at work.

My good friend and colleague, Mairi, was exhausted after doing chores at home and had hurt her back. We had only arrived at work when she told me she did not know if she could carry on working that day. I pulled a chair into a stock-room and gave her a ten-minute healing before we were due to start our shift. When I put my hands near her I could feel that she virtually had no energy within her. Straight away I could feel 'them upstairs' working on her back and giving her a boost of energy. I was able to readvise her, as I was given a vision of her working in her garden and what had caused her sore back. When I was busy suturing a woman in a room an hour later she came, banging on the door excitedly: "I just had to tell you - it's like night and day!" She couldn't believe how much energy she had and that her back was better. The healing session enabled her to carry on working for the rest of the shift. Mairi told Margaret, our team-leader, what I had done. Margaret joked with me, telling me she had been working with me all week with a sore back and didn't realise I could have helped her. I laughed, then pulled up a chair to help her, too.

Occasionally, I receive phone calls from family and friends who ask for distance-healing sessions. It may be difficult for some people to understand the concept of healing vibrations being able to reach people through time and space. I first learnt of energy manipulation and projection in my early teens by reading books written by the great healer, Betty Shine. When Betty was alive, she advised people to think of her and they would receive her help. I am sure she is helping even more people now she is in Spirit. She highlighted that we are able to link with souls in the afterlife and with people living on Earth when we are awake and when we are asleep, regardless of whether we have an awareness of doing it or not.

I have had many vivid dreams about helping others. I will never know if those experiences were real or not or if they related to my past or future. One sticks out more than most to the point that I could paint a picture of it. A brightness shone on the water as it waved with the tide. I caught glimpses of houses barely visible under the water. Then I witnessed bewildered people walk out of the deep water as they followed the contours of the hills. For a minute, my logical mind wondered how people could have survived the flood and walked out of the water the way they did. I became aware of being slightly in the distance, to the left of the people but on the right as I watched the scene. I was a few feet above them, guiding them home.

I have been told dreams in colour can be real, but black and white ones are usually just the mind processing data. There is so much we don't know about our minds and our dreams, and it would be impossible to know for sure if they are memories of events or just our imagination. For now, we can only surmise and learn through what our dreams tell us. There are many books on dream interpretations which contain varied teaching on the matter. This is because dreams are personal. They can mean one thing to one person and something completely different to another. Reading about other people's experience of dreams and psychic events may help to bridge the gap of the unknown.

look about him. I gave him the benefit of the doubt and sat chatting to him. Before long, he asked if I wanted to spend a couple of nights with him on his boat. I had had enough of men treating me this way. He seemed to be out of touch with his spiritual side so the scorpion in me began having fun with him. I told him I worked with energy and cried out: "I just love hugging trees!" By the end of the conversation, I'm sure, he thought I was a raving lunatic. He made his excuses and scampered to the pub toilets, never to be seen again.

For a few weeks, I dated another guy who was an accountant, until he began displaying strange behaviour. When I was in his room I could see female belongings in a bag so wondered who else was in his life. He told me he was helping a friend who was a member of the AA. The amount of empty wine and spirit bottles stacked high in his shed had me wondering whether he had many drunken times with this woman or if it was just him who had the problem. I stayed over at his house a few times, but for some reason he needed to explain that the female clothes in his spare-room wardrobe belonged to his sister. He had put on my silky night dress and danced about in it so the penny dropped. This man liked to dress up in woman's clothing and perhaps had a drink problem.

I was not judgmental, because I understand that when we are in true spirit form we are not in a human male or female body. We are made up of a kind of female and male energy called Yin and Yang. We may be composed more of one kind of energy than the other. Incidentally, Yin and Yang are also categorised as many other opposing things like hot and cold and wet and dry. People can get confused in the body they are currently in due to having past life memories of being the opposite sex or they generally have more of the opposing spiritual energy.

I knew my friendship with this man was over when he hung his Territorial Army uniform on his hall-way door un-ironed. He told me he was going to the barracks straight away and I was to leave. I wondered whom he was trying to kid. I was an ex-army wife and knew army guys would not go to the base with a uniform in that state. There was always the possibility that he had another woman in his life, but judging by his behaviour, I doubted it. Regardless of what it was all about - thankfully, this door shut fast behind me.

I gave dating of all kinds a miss for a while – then, one day, I got a message out of the blue from a guy called Andy from the Highlands. He was tall, dark-haired and looked like a young John Gordon, otherwise known as Gordon John Sinclair who starred in 'Gregory's Girl.' Andy lived up north, near where my mum and step-dad Bert were living. My parents had bought a house to be by the sea and to be near my brother David and his family. I had planned to join my family up north so began talking to Andy. We met in a car park half-way between where he was staying and my house and he followed me to my local pub where we had lunch. It was his birthday, so I gave him a Birthday card out of politeness. Since we seemed to hit it off, I asked him if he wanted to continue the date over drinks at a pub in town. We sat in a pub until it closed, chatting away. He said he was down in my area for another day, and subsequently we ended up on a full weekend date.

During our courtship, I travelled to Dingwall where Andy stayed and he travelled down to visit me. I had no idea I would end up dating a man whose granddad owned a sweetie factory that made the Kidd puff candy I used to love when I was young. William Kidd and Sons Sweetie Factory closed down when a compulsory purchase order was placed on his establishment. The Council's plan to build a road on the factory grounds never materialised. I often ask Andy why he doesn't set up the factory again, but he tells me there is too much opposition and red tape involved.

Before long, we ended up buying a house together in the Highlands, because it was half-way between Andy's work and where my mum lived. We began to integrate ourselves into village life even though I was still commuting to work in the Central Belt. I worked bank shifts in the two local hospitals as I planned to work at either of them in the future. It was not long before we thought about getting married, so we booked a church overlooking the sea and a Hotel for a meal and reception. My mum worked hard doing all the flowers. The church and reception hall were transformed with her flower arrangements. My Nana had loved cream roses when she was alive so there were beautiful cream roses decorated with teal ribbons and diamantes everywhere. My mum's sister made all the cream and teal invitations and stationery for the wedding. We laughed, saying we could have had a wedding package business with my mum's beautiful flower arranging, my aunts' talent for stationary, Natalie's flare for fashion and my ability to give calming healings, facials and massage therapies. I wore a decorative ivory silky wedding dress, and all the male members of the wedding party wore Highland kilt outfits. My mum's friend had a lovely car so it was decorated for the car-ride up to the church. David's eldest son played the bagpipes as I entered the church. Charlie's youngest son played an assortment of music on his electric guitar, while Andy and I signed the marriage certificate. Andy and I walked hand and hand out of the church to my favourite song which my Papa Hamilton used to play on his accordion: 'Highland Cathedral'.

We had bought a brown cocker spaniel puppy with a white chest a few weeks before we were married. His pedigree name 'Brambles Boy' was not suitable so we named him Harvey. He was too young to go into a kennel so we had to take him with us on honeymoon when we went for a week's holiday in the Gairloch. I was extremely happy at this time, but I am only realising now that I took my children out of their home without asking them what they thought about my re-marrying and moving up north. I believed my children were growing up and I needed someone in my life when they had flown the nest. Colin was angry with me so refused to move up north with us and went to stay with his dad. Kevin was already living up north with his partner and Natalie came to stay with me. Things seemed too good to be true for around eight weeks, and they were.

Before we were married, I had a miscarriage and then we were happy when I was pregnant again. Due to my age I opted to have an amniocentesis test. This test involved the doctor taking fluid from around the baby to check for abnormalities. During the procedure, I was looking away so I could not see what the doctor was doing. When he was ready, Andy piped up: “Oh, that’s a big needle!” I turned to Andy and scolded him: “You’re not helping!” I was surprised that I hardly felt the needle go in but was aware there was a slight chance of miscarriage after the procedure, so I rested up for a few days. When the initial test result came back, I was told all was normal and not to worry as everything would be fine. But it wasn’t fine. The full result showed that our baby had a chromosome problem which meant he would not survive the duration of the pregnancy. The doctor told us it was very rare for a test to come back mosaic so had not expected that result.

I stood in a maternity unit in a corner room – out of sight, with a pill in my hand. I flinched for a while as I knew to take the pill meant I would be starting the journey to end my unborn child’s doomed life. There were no positive outcomes to choose from. My thoughts turned to what the baby would have to endure if I could not swallow the pill. My heart sank as it slipped down my throat. Once the decision was made, a huge weight seemed to lift from me. I left for home to wait events. I was glad there was morphine to get me through the procedure of birthing my baby and the blessing we had to name him Matthew Robert. There was no morphine to help me walk out of the hospital with a baby memorial box instead of a baby or to help us stand over my son’s grave while we watched his little white coffin lower into the ground. For a short time, I wondered how I was going to continue my work as a midwife when I could not stomach the sight of pregnant women after my loss. Losing our baby was a very difficult time for us. It hit Andy more, because Matthew was his first baby. Burying your child is hard no matter what age or how it came to be, so saying ‘hello’ and ‘goodbye’ to our son floored us.

Andy and I both got a psychic reading when I was pregnant with Matthew. I should have clicked when Andy told me that the psychic medium predicted he would be a dad in two years’ time. I thought the woman was not up to scratch if she could not tell I was already pregnant with Matthew. She was indeed correct, because I became pregnant again only to lose that pregnancy. Then, I finally conceived my youngest son. Women used to be advised to wait before embarking on another pregnancy after experiencing a miscarriage, but I was not young. My fertile period was running out on the clock. After I lost Matthew, I suffered great pain which resulted in the need for me to have surgery. Most women who are in their forties are advised to have their ovaries removed should they experience problems with them. A kind consultant appreciated my wish to try for another baby so expelled a large amount of fluid from one and untwisted the other. Without his help, I would not have my young son in my life today.

For reasons I did not understand at the time, I had the knowledge of the moment my children were conceived. I noticed this more with my youngest son, because what I experienced the moment of his conception was more profound. I can only explain it as a clunk sensation, like a locking of two parts as I saw what I can only describe as an explosive blue spark within my mind. I turned to Andy and told him: "It's done." Spirit taught me the timing of a spirit or soul joining the human body varies as this is decided by the spirit alone. The complete merging of the soul does not usually occur till the moment of birth. This is when the soul's guardian angel releases them to allow to them to have free will and be accountable for their own actions.

I attended my local GP surgery where a doctor scanned me. He told me there was no heartbeat so I was to go home and await events. I explained that I had long commutes on the A9, had a bad obstetric history and so requested another scan. The next week, I was discussing my situation with two midwives in my local hospital. I was busy trying to arrange a date to have the products of conception removed while they scanned my abdomen. The midwives looked at me, smiled and pointed to a small blob on the screen with a flickering heart beat. My mum and Andy's mum were sitting in the waiting-room quietly after having a rant with each other in the corridor about me being too old to be having a baby, and that after what Andy and I had been through it was for the best. I walked into the waiting area and gave them the good news. They both sat with their mouths wide open, flabbergasted. It was not quite the reaction I was expecting and probably the wrong one to be given in a room full of pregnant onlookers.

I fell pregnant around the time I got married so I was eight weeks pregnant with Andy's second son when we decided to go down to Glasgow for his best friend's big birthday party. We were sitting in his parents' living-room, chatting after eating supper. We were just about to get ready for the party when Andy started behaving oddly. His skin appeared grey and he was making a funny noise. I realised something was very wrong so dragged him off the settee onto the floor. I shouted to Andy's mum to come through to the living-room as Andy's dad could not calm himself enough to dial for an ambulance. I had to speak clearly and in phrases so Andy's mum could be calm enough to dial for help. I checked Andy's airway, thinking his tongue might have rolled back blocking his airway or he might be choking on some food. I must have done it wrongly, because he bit my finger a little. He had a pulse which was going fast and he had lost consciousness. When he came round, his colour returned to normal so I put him into the recovery position. The Ambulance crew arrived when Andy was conscious, but because he had no history of having a medical condition and because he was still confused, they took him to Monklands hospital to be checked over. The potassium in his body was found to be out of balance so he was kept in hospital overnight to be observed and given intravenous fluids.

When the doctor came to discharge Andy the next day, I questioned him about what he thought had happened, but he had no idea. I told the doctor I was concerned as we had a long journey home, with a risk of no phone signal if something were to happen. When we were back at home, I felt very queasy with morning sickness. I told Andy that I felt too out of sorts to be travelling back down to work that week. I was commuting from the Highlands to my work every four days but had the intention of giving up work and the long commute after the baby was born.

Andy and I were sitting in our living-room, chilling while watching television and Natalie was busy in her room, when Andy started making a strider noise again. I shouted for Natalie to call an ambulance, but she said the number kept ringing out. The operator was not answering the emergency call, so I dragged Andy onto the floor. He was turning a dull-grey colour. His circulation was failing and this time, it was much worse than during the previous episode. I commenced giving him CPR and continued for a few minutes while I shouted at him: "Don't you leave me!" Eventually, the female operator asked my daughter what the matter was. She must have been able to hear me counting out the compressions over the phone.

Natalie took Harvey out of the living-room and started giving the operator all the details for Andy to get help. The ambulance crew took eight minutes to arrive and by that time I was tired from thumping on his chest and breathing air into him. The ambulance crew asked me to keep giving CPR until they were set up to help him. The doctor sited a venflon into Andy's hand and gave some intravenous drugs, while one of the ambulance crew placed pads on Andy's chest and used the cardio defibrillator on him. They were still struggling to bring him back after shocking him twice. It was at this point that I fell to pieces and stood back to let them work. They managed to get him semi-conscious enough to get him ready to be transferred to hospital. I phoned Andy's mum to tell her what had happened, because I had no idea if he was going to pull through or not. The ambulance crew had to shock him again in the ambulance. They managed to bring him around enough for him to shout at them for hurting his ribs. "Don't blame me, mate. That was your wife!" one of the crew said.

Natalie and I followed the Ambulance at a high speed. I got angry with some car drivers as they must have been able to see the blue flashing lights and hear the sirens, but they did not get out of the way to let the ambulance through. The road from my town to Inverness Hospital was not a dual-carriage road so I started shouting at cars even though they could not hear me: "Get out of the way!" I was livid – how could they not understand the ambulance needed to get to the hospital quickly with a very sick man? I reached the hospital and parked my car, not knowing if Andy would be alive or dead or if he would be physically or mentally impaired. I found him in the accident and emergency room, propped up on a transport trolley with wires attached to him everywhere.

He was moved to a critical ward where he was to stay for a few weeks. Andy told me months later that he had had no idea that his mum had been sitting in a chair beside him most of the time. He has no memory of the event at all. We still had no idea what had happened to him, until a consultant asked me to go into a room to discuss it. I was told only one out of around two hundred people survive ventricular fibrillation events so Andy was extremely lucky that I had been around to help him. It would have been a very different story if I had gone to work that week and taken Natalie down with me to her dad's as I usually did. The consultant joked, saying he would get me into his department to teach his staff CPR, because what I did must have been effective. He continued to tell us if Andy had died we would never have known what had happened, because there were no visible defects with his heart. When he has an attack, his heart goes so fast it quivers and does not pump enough blood and oxygen to his body.

There was no way of knowing when he would have another attack, if any. If he was to have another attack it could kill him, so he needed an internal cardio defibrillator (ICD) implanted as soon as they could perform the surgery. He spent a week attached to leads and was not allowed out of the ward where they could give him continual monitoring. He had to have the surgery before he was permitted to go home and recover. He had some coordination problems which were resolved and has some memory loss from time to time, but other than that he has come out the other end better than we all thought he would.

It takes great courage to accept the loss of your state of health and for Andy, the worst for him was when he had to accept the loss of his job as a BOC consultant. He had run a one-man site in Inverness and was respected by many people in businesses all around the north of Scotland and Skye. I am sure the customers miss him as much as he misses them. The loss of his job meant I had to keep commuting from the Highlands to my work, up and down the notorious A9 road every four or five days. Andy got depressed about not having his job and the lifestyle he loved. During an argument he shouted: "I wish you had left me!" "I would have if the will had been signed!" I replied. He dragged me to a lawyer and got a will sorted out the next day, but I believe he has a machine which will keep him going a lot longer than me and the people around him.

Andy, Natalie and I were in my car in the town of Inverness after a leisurely walk around the shops. Andy was not permitted to drive until he was deemed medically fit so I was driving. I pulled the handbrake on as we were stopped by a red light at a set of traffic lights. Out of the corner of my eye, I saw Andy slump forward on the passenger seat. I watched him for a couple of seconds. I was about to drag him out of the car to start CPR when I witnessed his ICD giving him a shock. His body jumped up and he came around wondering what had just happened. I raced him to the hospital where the specialist confirmed he had been shocked back by the device. He was given a higher prescription of drugs to help him with his heart condition and stop him having further episodes. He appreciates the seriousness of having to take the tablets, but they cause troublesome side-effects which he is still trying to accept and come to terms with.

When extreme circumstances happen in our lives, it sometimes means we have to do extreme things to keep afloat. I was twenty-seven weeks pregnant, driving four hours every four or five days to and from work. I was experiencing some niggles which was not exactly a good thing as I had a grade four placenta praevia, which in laymen's terms means my placenta was in the wrong place. This condition could cause me to bleed to death if I did not have immediate help should I begin to bleed profusely. I had a family to support with a mortgage and bills to pay, so I had to continue working regardless of my health. I was able to go off sick from work as soon as changes were made to the rules relating to sick-pay while pregnant.

I had to spend six weeks as an inpatient in a maternity unit until the agreed date to have a caesarean section. I missed Natalie a great deal at this time, because she had to stay with my mum for those six weeks. Andy came into theatre when I was having the surgery so was by my side when little Cameron calmly came into the world. Cameron had some slight breathing difficulties, which can happen when a baby is born around thirty-seven weeks so had to stay in the special baby-care unit overnight. My mum helped me get out of bed and shower the next day, before she took me in a wheelchair to see Cameron. I stroked his little face to let him know I was with him. The early days with a new baby were exhausting and I felt guilty for not spending the same amount of time with Natalie, especially as she was beginning to show signs of being unwell. She was not the baby of the family any more but unknown to me then, needed me more than ever.

OUR GIRL

Natalie

When I look back on the life of my daughter I think of her as being all ages – a baby, a child, a teenager, a woman and now a highly evolved spirit guiding me on my Earth journey and helping me overcome my grief.

My pregnancy had gone without a hitch, but her birth was a little more eventful. Six days after my due date I had not felt her move for a day or two. while I sat in the maternity unit, a doctor came and sat beside me. He looked at my huge bump and said: "You are very pregnant." He arranged for me to have a scan and to have my labour induced the next morning. My husband hugged Kevin and Colin while they watched the sonographer scan my abdomen. This was the moment we found out that a little girl was joining our family.

My body responded quickly to the medication inducing my labour on New Year's Eve in 1994. I rocked myself away from the pain in the antenatal ward with my mum and husband beside me. I had a lot of pressure, until I felt a large pop which gave me relief: "Ah, that's better." The midwife took a little while to check on me, and when she did, she went into automatic panic mode. I thought, *I am not worried and not in pain so why was she worried*? She bunged me onto a hospital bed, made me say a quick goodbye to my mum and rushed me down to the labour suite. After a short period of bearing down, my daughter was born into the world with 'a petted lip'. We called her Natalie as I had always loved this name and gave her the middle name of Jane after Bert's mum, who was a fine lady.

I was actively bleeding so I asked the midwife to give Natalie to her dad. I was mesmerised looking at her little foot hanging over his arm, feeling an immense surge of love for her. I was oblivious to the emergency bell sounding for more staff to come and help the midwife with my post-partum haemorrhage. After the emergency was over, my husband looked at me, then at our daughter and said: "That will be some twenty-first birthday party!" Natalie was taken to the post-natal ward overnight so the staff could look after her while I spent the night in the labour ward being given four units of blood and intravenous fluid to replace the three litres of blood I lost. Shortly before commencing the blood transfusion, I felt faint but so happy, light and carefree. The bells for the new year rang out and the staff cheered while I lay alone in the darkness hooked up to drips and machines, unable to sleep without my baby beside me. I was on cloud nine as I had my beautiful two boys and a much-wanted daughter.

Natalie loved to dance in my arms and giggled when I sang to her. She had chronic colic so spent her first few months crying and drawing her knees up no matter what I tried. She cried and had temper tantrums most days until she was five years old as she wanted to be the boss. The boys would shout in tandem: "Natalie, shut up!" When she stomped up the stairs one by one, the boys shouted: "You missed one!" She would climb down a few steps to stomp the step they said she had missed. From the time she was four years old, I had to lay out a choice of three outfits each morning on her bed so she could be the one to choose what clothes she was going to wear. She was very young when I had to stop buying her clothes if she was not with me to pick them. In a reading with a medium called Diane White, Natalie apologised for being such hard work when she was young.

I had the emotional turmoil of losing her for half an hour when she was two years old. I had already had some heart-wrenching experiences with Colin as he was prone to run off and disappear for a while. Colin was the same age as little James Bulger when he was taken so the fear of child abduction lay heavy on my mind. I bought a lightweight buggy to strap him down when he was three years old. However, this scenario was different. We were at home, Natalie was only two and there was no reason for her to be anywhere but home. My heart beat faster, tears welled up in my eyes, despair and desperation crept in. My walk turned into a sprint as I looked everywhere for her. I thought *if this was a short glimpse of what families have to suffer their whole lives when a child goes missing then I don't know how they can keep on breathing*. After fifteen minutes of searching, I knocked on my neighbours' doors, asking if they could help find her.

I was so relieved when she appeared at the livingroom window in my friend Liz's house. She was standing on the large window ledge unaware of my anguish. I tried to get her to open the window, but she just kept waving at me. Liz worked in our local corner shop so I was able to run and tell her Natalie was locked inside her house. I ran back to keep an eye on her from outside until Liz appeared. I had a close friendship with Liz, and our children were used to walking into each other's houses to play. Natalie had sneaked in through Liz's back-door and gone up to one of her children's rooms to play while Liz and her family had gone out the front-door.

Liz looked after Natalie on a few occasions when I did drama gigs. I was five months pregnant with Natalie when I played the part of a young girl who was concealing a pregnancy in a murder mystery event, so Natalie had a claim to fame about being on the stage at a young age. She was also the youngest to begin riding her bike. I came home from my work to find a two-and-a-half-year-old tearing up and down the street on her two-wheeled bike minus stabilisers. Liz had taught her a few hours before I got home. She was advanced for her age at most things, because she had older brothers she tried to keep up with.

Natalie had a pretty all-in-pink clothes phase, then a longer tomboy-football-and-rugby-outfit phase. I had two boys, but she was the only one in our household who liked football. She played in her school team. She was playing in a match when another six-year-old girl kicked her instead of the ball. I was so immersed in the game that I temporarily lost my senses and shouted: "Kick her back!" I hid under my coat, wondering where that came from.

I was paranoid about losing her, especially as she had beautiful blonde hair, fair skin and deep-blue eyes. Before she went on holiday abroad with her dad, I warned her to stay beside him. I was beside myself. I had a feeling something may happen so counted the days till she got back. She later told me that she had asked a shop-keeper if he had any of her favourite football team tee-shirts. The man told her he had some in the back and walked with her to the back of his shop. At that point Natalie's dad walked up beside her. When her dad appeared, the man changed his mind, telling her that – actually – he didn't have any teeshirts. Natalie believed this man had acted strangely and was glad her dad had stayed close to her.

She loved going on holiday and was never short of friends to go on holiday with. Her favourite holiday was when she went to Ibiza with a large group of her friends. She acquired the love of holidaying abroad when she first went with her school friend Heather and Heather's family. Heather told me the two of them had been at the airport when Natalie decided to try and get an alcoholic drink. She was on a mission when she punted up at the bar and cheekily asked for two glasses of vodka and cola. The bar man looked at the two young girls and said: "Can I see your identification?" "We don't have any", Natalie replied. The man looked at her as if she had two heads. On realising she was in an airport bar with her passport, she quickly retreated.

My mum owned a static caravan in Pease Bay Caravan Park, just off the A1 near the border of Scotland and England for many years. She and Bert lived there most of the time so we spent many weekends and week-long holidays there. Natalie loved the beach. I thought she was going to be heavily into water sports when she was older, because she loved trying to ride the waves with her little surf-board. She was in the sea wearing her wet suit from March till it got too cold at the end of summer.

She loved an adventure, so when I asked her if she wanted to go on a road trip she jumped at the chance. We drove from Stirling to Gloucester to buy and pick up a Dandy Trailer Tent. We stopped off overnight at a campsite and slept in a tent, watching a film with my DVD machine. After that, we enjoyed a short holiday at a caravan site in England with our new trailer tent – we played tennis, kicked a ball around, went for a walk along a canal and then ate at a nice Hotel before settling down for the night to watch some more films. On the way back, she was in fits of laughter, watching me trying to reverse the trailer without previous training. I resorted to finding places to go around in a circle to avoid reversing when we took a wrong turn. We had the same sense of humour. She made me laugh when she was laughing at me. Someone had jutted in-front of us, making me swerve. I shouted at them: "Yah Nini-nani-noo-noo!" That then became our nickname for people who were being stupid.

Natalie's last family holiday with us was at Seton Sands near Edinburgh. We were blessed with warm sunny weather. We took Cameron to the park, played at the beach and lay under the sun by our caravan. We enjoyed some quality time together at the clubhouse, while Cameron played with other children. Natalie had a fear of spiders, and when one appeared in the caravan she jumped about like mad person, shouting at Andy and me to get it. While all this commotion was going on, three-year- old Cameron opened the caravan door and released his newly-bought Tiger balloon up into the sky. He became hysterical when it disappeared out of sight. We had to explain that his balloon had gone up into the sky beside all the clouds and the planes. Luckily, the vendors at the caravan site gave Cameron another balloon to end his temper tantrum. Months later, we all went to East Fortune Museum of Flight for a day trip. Cameron spotted a plane in the Museum which had a painting of a tiger resembling the balloon he lost months before. We laughed when he pointed at the plane and tried to climb up it, shouting: "My balloon will be in there!"

The time I have spent with my children has always been the best hours in my life. When my eldest children were young, I did not have the finances to take them on expensive days out or on holidays abroad. They seemed to be happy with trips to our local parks and occasional playtime in soft-play centres. We enjoyed going on weekly trips to the cinema with cheap family tickets. Out of the blue, the old cinema hall closed to make way for a multi-cinema complex out of town. This meant the family ticket price quadrupled overnight so was out of the price range for my single-parent wages. However, my children never complained about me giving them movie nights with carpet picnics at home instead.

Being a single parent meant I was always looking to cut corners to keep within a tight budget. My mum and Bert helped me with some bills I got and one day, Bert came into my living-room unexpectedly with a new television when mine was broken. Natalie was more expensive to keep; I guess girls generally are. The only expensive part of raising my boys was the regular hair cuts they needed. Then I had a brain wave of buying hair clippers. I placed a chair in-front of me and stood with the clippers in my hand beckoning the boys to sit down: "Right, who is first?" Kevin dashed out the door, but Colin was happy to be my first customer. I took one sweep at his exceptionally thick hair and the clippers stuck fast: "Oops!" Colin looked at me: "Really, Mum?" This then became their statement when I did or said crazy things. Poor Colin had to go to school wearing a hat until he got to the barbers for a proper hair cut. I am known for not reading instructions so had to apologise to him for not realising I needed to put oil into the clippers before I began. Kevin laughed at Colin for being so daft, allowing me to do that to him.

Kevin and Colin reminded me of how I used to cut corners with many of my DIY attempts. I tried my hand at tiling a wall one evening, only to be greeted in the morning with the full batch of tiles lying on the floor. In those days, I took advantage of many discounted DIY items. Kevin laughed about the time he had to lie down in the back of the car under a new door I bought at half-price. The boys never seemed to get upset with my cost- cutting measures, but Natalie was a different story.

She could always twist me around her little finger to get the things she wanted. She was a leader, not a follower. She started new fashions at school by mixing up her clothing to give a particular look. She began wearing waistcoats or thick band belts but got upset when all her friends copied her. I have no idea where she got the taste for fashionable clothing; it certainly wasn't from me. She used to parade in-front of me, going around in circles, asking me what I thought about her outfit. I had to tell her she was asking the wrong person: "Wait and ask your gran," I used to say.

She loved shopping for clothes, but our bank balances didn't. Kevin and Colin were much easier to dress as they were happy with anything I bought them, but Natalie wanted the best. She tried to convince me to buy a pair of jeans which cost seventy pounds. She gave the argument of how good the quality of the material was. She would not listen to me so I resolved to let her try the jeans on. She paraded around the changing room trying to convince me that they were a perfect fit. She eventually got the message that those jeans were not going home with her, so she ran to look at another pair priced at thirty pounds. "What about these then?" I gave her the look of '*no chance*' and took her over to a rail with sale items on. Similar jeans were half-price so she ended up happy with them along with a tee-shirt which was also in the sale. She walked out the shop merrily swinging a bag containing her new clothes, winning the day, because I had not intended to buy her anything.

Her appearance was important to her, especially when she had a long-term boyfriend at thirteen years old. I thought this was a bit young, but in hind-sight, I am glad she had this experience and lived her life to the full. She always said she did not want to grow up so I wonder if she knew deep down her time was short. She tried to pack so much into her life.

She had a few evenings when she drank alcohol with her friends but came home, so at least I knew she was safe. One night, though, she overstepped the mark. She came sneaking up the stairs of our house after a night out with her friends, obviously trying to avoid me. I was working on the computer in her room and when she entered the room and saw me, she stopped dead, relaxed her shoulders and gave a big sigh. "Have you been drinking, Natalie?" She looked at me, knowing there was no use in arguing and replied: "Aye." I stopped what I was doing to let her get to her bed and sleep it off.

She had pushed the boundaries too far so – as a result - she ended up being kept away from her friends for a few months to make her think about her behaviour. Her friends phoned her and asked: "What are you grounded for this time?" She was regularly kept indoors, away from her friends and all her antics with them if she did not comply with rules such as coming home at an agreed time and doing many more things that would take forever to list.

At school, her teacher told me that she was being disruptive in his class, so he moved her down to the front beside him, away from her friends. She was further reprimanded for all her friends moving to the front to be with her. She spent a year at Bannockburn High School, testing the boundaries and just wanting to mess around with her friends. I had to keep telling her off for her behaviour: "Pull your socks up, Natalie!" She would reply: "I hate you saying that." She was a star pupil when she first attended the school, but then she was getting out of control. She won the Top-Of-Her-Year award for cookery every year, except in the year she was mischievous. Her teachers described her as a pupil who had a 'zest for life'.

When she continued to be unruly at school, I moved her to The High School of Stirling, which was much further away. She lasted three days at the new school before she pleaded with me, promising to behave: "I'll pull my socks up, Mum, please let me go back!" I was a soft touch so let her go back to her old school. She suddenly began following my rules when I resorted to taking her mobile phone off her. I kicked myself for not thinking about that method sooner. She improved her grades and began acting more like the Natalie we knew and loved.

I don't know how many times she phoned me to pick her up after she had missed the last bus home from another village when visiting her friends or how many times she broke or lost her phone. She was the only person I knew who could drop a phone in a fire, down the toilet, sit on it and lose it in a park and on buses. One kind bus driver phoned me to go and retrieve it half-way through his route. During the time, when she could not bathe alone due to the risk of having a seizure, I sat with her. On one of these occasions, she dropped her new phone in the bath. She shrieked at me, telling me to get it. I scooped my hand in and grabbed it while she had her leg up out of the way. I asked her: "Why didn't you just pick it up?" "I didn't want to get electrocuted!" "Oh right," I laughed, "So it's okay for me to get electrocuted?"

I guess most parents will do what they can to help and protect their children. Things may inevitably happen so we can only warn them as best we can. I did not like the thought of my children smoking, but Kevin was an adult by then so there was not much I could do about it. My nextdoor neighbours smoked at their back door so when cigarette ends started appearing I got angry with Kevin and my neighbours for throwing the ends down. Kevin bought a tin bucket for all the ends to go in and went about picking them up. Poor Kevin got chucked out of our house to his dad's house for a while for smoking indoors after I found a Wellington boot full of cigarette ends and more under our three-piece suite. I was shocked that he did this, because he knew how much I detested the smell of cigarette smoke in the house. I gave him a huge lecture about how dangerous it is to smoke in the house. It was many years before I clicked. It must have been Natalie who smoked in the house. She was probably smoking at her bedroom window, throwing the ends into the back garden and hid them in her boot and under the settee.

I was outside, cleaning my car when I was trying to talk some sense into a thirteen-year-old Natalie: "What is it about smoking that you like?" "It helps me relax," she explained. I continued washing my car, shaking my head in frustration. I did not want to talk about it anymore. I was done trying to explain how bad it was for her health. She eventually stopped smoking a couple of years later without me saying a word.

After my apology, which will never be enough, I asked Kevin why he did not tell me what Natalie was up to. He replied: "I'm not a grass." I guess this is the price eldest siblings often have to pay, because they usually get the blame for most things until otherwise proven. He was regularly chastised for the messy state he kept his and Colin's room in. It took many years before I learned that Colin used to push his mess over to Kevin's side of the room and let his brother take the blame for it.

Kevin and Natalie had similar natures. They were both adventurous, full of fun and with a calm, caring side to them. Colin was often irritated by Kevin and Natalie's antics, because he has always been mature beyond his age. Natalie was the only one who shared my belief of life after death. We talked many times on the subject from when she was at a young age. As we were a single-parent family for fourteen years, she used to sleep beside me in my bed until she was in her teens, rather than sleep in her own bed. It was our special time when we used to discuss many things about life and our experiences. When she was around twelve years old she told me she sometimes saw little blue twinkling lights. I was able to reassure her, because I saw them, too. I explained to her that the lights were sparks of energy and most probably were the energy of our loved ones in spirit. She got a bit frightened and said: "I would jump a mile if I saw a ghost!" I tried to reassure her it would just be the energy of her spirit guide or our Nana and my dad staying close to her, looking after her.

When I was reading a book about the afterlife or alternative therapies in bed, she would always ask: "What are you reading?" Before I knew it, she would nab my book off me and be well engrossed in its contents. The same happened if I was relaxing with some healing music. She would nick the headphones off me and fall asleep while listening to the soothing sounds. We discussed what we may expect on the other side. We agreed when I died I would let her know I was still around, and then she surprised me when she said she would do the same if she went first.

I guess our close relationship began to lessen when I made plans to move up north and marry Andy. She never let it show that she was unhappy living in a small village; above everything else, she wanted to stay with me. She attended the local Academy for a few days but could not settle there. She was permitted to go to college when she was fifteen instead of school so began studying a few higher subjects at Inverness College. The only subject she talked about was Higher Human Biology because she liked her tutor and the way the subject was taught. I was able to help her with this subject so she managed to get high marks in her class exams. Then, for some reason, she began to fall away from college. She would take money for the bus fare but would not go to college. When I found out about her skipping college, I was more upset about her thinking she could not come to me and tell me how she was feeling. We agreed she should try to keep going with two of her classes, Higher Human Biology being one of them.

By this time, she was complaining of being tired, having sore heads and feeling dizzy. I took her to see a doctor a few times and was told she had imbalances from ear infections and labyrinthitis. I took her to further doctor appointments when she suffered from dizziness to the extent that I had to sleep beside her. She felt as if she was going to fall out of her bed and had to hold onto things when she felt at her worst. She was unable to walk around the town during her lunch breaks as she felt she had to hold onto her friends to stay upright. The doctors didn't seem too concerned so Natalie continued to live with the symptoms. She began spending more days at home than at college.

One day, when she managed the car journey to college, I had just returned home after dropping her off when I got a call from her lecturer. I rushed back to the college to find Natalie lying on the floor with a first-aid lecturer beside her. She could not stand up and the noise of the class was too much stimulation for her. I took her straight to the doctor's clinic for an emergency appointment where I asked the doctor to investigate her symptoms. I pleaded: "But this is not like her! What about a scan?" Natalie was holding on tight to her chair, her pupils were tiny and she felt faint. She called it her 'Swimmy' feeling. The GP believed Natalie was suffering from depression and panic attacks so prescribed her anti-depressants. I had previously requested bloods to be taken at an earlier emergency appointment to see if a reason could be found for her feeling tired all the time and sleeping through the day. Natalie told the doctor she didn't feel depressed, but the tablets seemed to suppress her brain activity and symptoms to a level Natalie could live with.

After a while, she stopped going to college altogether. She didn't have many friends where we lived and missed her boyfriend and friends in Stirling. She could not adjust to life up north and eventually moved back down to stay with her dad. Natalie moving back down to Stirling helped me to get used to her not being around. I often wonder if this was part of the larger plan to help me get over losing her. Her family and friends in Stirling must have been used to her being away for periods of time and may have felt this way, too, when she was up north with me. I missed her greatly but understood she needed to spread her wings so let her go and do what she wanted. She liked being with many people, travelling and living life to the full. The quiet life of a small village was not for her.

Natalie lived between her dad's house and mine. She accompanied me on many of the commutes from The Highlands to the Central Belt of Scotland. She played cd compilations on the car cd player she made specially for the journeys. Eventually, after listening to her rave music at full pelt for an hour or so I would say to her: "Natalie! Do you have to?" She would look at me and smile then pick a cd with the kind of music she knew we both liked. The A9 road in Scotland is known to be notorious where many people are killed in road accidents due to people speeding and making poor judgements when overtaking other vehicles. This route is open and unsheltered in many parts so can be dangerous in the winter.

It was snowing heavily and the road was compacted with snow and ice when we were travelling north. This in itself was not as dangerous as the drivers infront of us. I kept well back from the other vehicles, but I had to continually use my handbrake to avoid them when they slammed their breaks on. I began to wish Natalie was not in the car with me. I had a good amount of experience driving in snow and ice after having lived in Germany and was not usually frightened to drive in these conditions. This night, however, was very different as I began to get fearful. I had heard of white-outs but I had never experienced one. The view in-front of us was like a sheet of paper; there were no contours or shapes of any kind. Natalie didn't say anything, but the fact that she was quiet let me know she felt fearful, too. I slowly edged into what I could just make out was a lay-by. Before the speed limit was raised for heavy goods vehicles, they were a pain on the A9 as they slowed other vehicles down. Motorists tried to overtake them and got hurt in the process. On this occasion, I was so glad to see one. I could see that the driver of the lorry who crawled past me was also having trouble seeing ahead but he was higher up and had bigger and brighter lights than I had. I pulled out and slowly followed him until he got us much further north, where the road became clear and bright with lights. I overtook him on a dual road and flashed my lights many times to thank him for helping us get home that night. It was after this experience that I thought something had to change. Driving on the A9 every four or five days in the winter was no fun anymore.

Natalie began working in Greggs Baker shop in Stirling so her shifts did not always coincide with mine. She began travelling by bus or train to visit us. It was during one of these commutes I had to drive her to Inverness train station. She was taking so long with straightening her long blonde hair in readiness to meet her boyfriend in Stirling that I had to shout at her: "Natalie, if we don't go now you will miss your train!" It was always 'Drama, Drama' with Natalie, but only for the people around her. She never seemed to get bothered or stressed about things and calmly climbed into my car and messed about with the radio dial to get a music station she liked. "There's never a decent radio station up here, Mum", she said while popping one of her cds into the car cd player. I had to drive like a mad woman, overtaking cars on the half-hour journey. I was bedraggled by the time we reached the train station. I grabbed her suitcase and chucked her and her case onto the train just before it pulled out of the station. We had made it by the skin of our teeth. Natalie sat in a cheap first-class seat I managed to wangle, cheerily waving goodbye to me while someone was pouring her a cup of tea and handing her a newspaper.

Natalie began visiting less when she was working so I was unable to monitor her symptoms. She was so far away, but I hoped she was getting better when she was living in her dad's house. She spent a great deal of her time with her friends and talked to me about her plans to move into a flat with one of them. She had been having driving lessons with a family friend and with my brother Charlie, who were both driving instructors. She phoned me to tell me how excited she was to be sitting her driving test in a few days' time as she had always wanted to have her own car. She was staying overnight at one of her friend's house in readiness to go to T in the Park with her friend and her friend's family the next day.

It's Cancer

She never made it to T in the Park, because she suffered a seizure that night. Her friend's mum told her it was probably only a temperature fit. Natalie phoned me when I was at my work the next day. I hit the roof but calmed myself so I could continue the rest of the conversation without worrying her: "You have to go to the doctor immediately, Natalie." She promised she would get her dad to take her before she put the phone down. The doctor sent her for a scan straight away and that is when I got the phone call. I had just finished transferring my patient to the postnatal ward around four o'clock, when Colin managed to get me on the labour ward phone: "Mum, where have you been? We have been trying to get a hold of you for ages!" I knew from Colin's tone something really bad was going on. "What, Colin?" I just wanted him to blurt it out. "Natalie is in hospital; they have found a shadow on her brain." I fell to my knees while holding onto the phone. My mind was numb while Colin continued to tell me what the doctors had said, where she was, who was with her and what they planned to do. I ran to get my bag and stood bolt upright in-front of the labour ward Charge Midwife and asked if I could leave. I began walking away before the reply came as I was not taking 'no' for an answer.

I raced to the hospital in Larbert to find Natalie lying on a bed in a corner room of a ward. I ran to give her a long cuddle and wipe her tears before wiping my own. After we calmed down, I was taken outside the room and told that she had a mass measuring at least six centimetres wide in her brain. She was to have a detailed scan and further treatment in the specialist unit of what was known then as the Southern General Hospital. I phoned my mum and made sure someone was with her when I told her the bad news. Then I phoned my mother-in-law who I lived with when I was working and asked her to bring me my suitcase with my clothes and toiletries and to tell Andy where I was. I was going to stay in the hospital with Natalie; I was going nowhere. Natalie and I lay together all night on her hospital bed cuddling. She got upset, saying she didn't want to die. I reminded her of all our chats of the afterlife and not to be scared either way. I told her not to think about that - she needed to think about getting better. She wiped her tears and bravely said: "Yip, if it's Cancer, I'm going to kick its butt!"

It is hard for me to recollect every detail of Natalie's journey as part of me lived in a state of shock from the time I received the phone call at work until well after I lost her. There are other people in her family who could probably recall every detail, but I can't. Natalie had scans which showed that she needed immediate treatment.

Many doctors took great interest in her case because her tumour was the largest brain tumour they had ever seen. A wonderful Teenage Cancer Specialist Nurse helped Natalie through Natalie's whole journey.

Natalie's journey began by having a major operation to debulk her tumour. It was not a mass which was separate from her brain cells. It was embedded and was part of her brain so she was warned they would take away as much as they could, but she may have physical or mental damage when she woke up from the surgery. She calmly told the theatre nurse she understood what procedure she was having while being wheeled into the anaesthetic room. I hugged her until she fell asleep. I was beside myself. I met the rest of the family and sobbed: "She shouldn't have to go through this. She is too young to be going through this!" At seventeen and a half, Natalie was being a lot braver than I was.

Natalie wakened with a scar just behind her hair line from one side of her head to the other. She shouted at the male theatre nurse: "What have you done to me?" She was in a lot of pain so the nurse gave her a shot of morphine and then he asked her how she feeling. "I'm fine, how are you?" was her chirpy reply. She had never had morphine before so she was flying on the pain relief. After the operation, I was permitted to stay with her in her hospital room to help care for her. We waited to see if there were any problems with her mental and physical abilities. She had a shunt in her brain to help reduce the swelling as it could cause another seizure. Her movements were slow and her knees jerky when she began to walk. There was a fridge packed full of all the food she fancied so she ended up walking to the fridge frequently to see what she wanted to snack on. While she was there, a little boy made her smile. He stared at all the staples in her head and shouted: "Cool!" as if she was someone out of a super-hero film. She was a superhero to me. Her face and head were so swollen and bruised it saddened me. She allowed me to take a picture of her so she could see how much better she would become as time went on.

We had no idea of the journey ahead of us but learned quickly that Natalie needed urgent intensive radiotherapy or chemotherapy very soon after her operation. The specialists regularly hold meetings to discuss each patient's case. They decide together what kind of treatment is best for each one. The result of the biopsy of

Natalie's tumour was available so she was given all the information regarding both methods of treatment and was to make her own choice of what she wanted. The specialists did not know what the best option was for her. She was under eighteen and her brain was still growing so radiotherapy would not normally be an option for her. The seriousness of her condition meant she was given the choice. The consultant phoned me while I was at work to verify that I understood all the issues with both options. He wanted me to go over it all again with Natalie so she could make an informed choice.

Natalie decided to have six weeks of daily radiotherapy treatment, excluding weekends. She wanted to be well quicker than the chemo could make her so she could drive a car and go on a planned holiday to Ibiza with her friends. She had to have a specially made mask which fitted over her face and head. It was to help her keep still and pin- pointed exactly where the arch radiotherapy would beam over and around the areas of her brain. These were areas which could still contain cancerous cells. She had developed a fear of needles, therefore, my concentration was on calming her down so staff could site a venflon in her hand. When she was settled and ready to go into the machine for the first time, I caught sight of her white trainers on her feet. I was overwhelmed by the sight of my child wearing children's shoes going through a scary machine which might save her life. This sight made my tears fall, but they were wiped away before she came back to me. She listened to her favourite music while under the machine to help take her mind off what she was going through. Every time I heard her music, knowing she was under the machine, my heart twisted and tightened. I watched other sick people of all ages going in one by one to the radiotherapy room. This experience humbled me, reminding me what was important in life and what was not.

Natalie became exhausted near the end of her six weeks' treatment so I had to fetch a chair to wheel her back to the car. She sat on a couch beside an office which offered counselling while she waited for me to get a wheelchair as all the other seats were occupied. A slim woman came out of the office and shouted at her for sitting on the couch which was only meant for her clients. We were taken aback by her attitude but did not waste our energy to tell her Natalie was a client. People may look well, but we sometimes have no idea what is going on in their lives.

The part of Natalie's brain which was affected was to do with her personality. We noted at times she had some problems with her short-term memory and a very slight change in her zappy nature but overall, she came out the other end of her treatment pretty well. Her physical movements improved quickly, so did her confidence in kicking her Cancer's butt. She hid her scar with head bands until hair grew over it and gracefully accepted the round imperfect indent on the bone of the left side of her forehead where she had had her operation. During the nights I spent with her when she was recovering from her surgery, she told me about a very vivid dream she had. She was walking on a board-walk with her Nana until she began walking away from her. Her Nana asked where she was going and she pointed to a big banner which read: 'Getting better.' "I'm going over there, Nana", she said. Natalie had every confidence in this dream coming true and I guess it did for a while. I often wonder if she was destined to die at that time but had been given grace to live a little longer.

She requested an investigation into the care she received by her GP practice. When she went to another GP practice to collect her medical notes a doctor said: "If everyone got a scan then those who need one would not get one." This upset Natalie and me as he was speaking to a young seventeen-year old girl who had Cancer with a late diagnosis because she had not received one sooner.

Natalie spoke out in support of the Sunday Post's Fighting Chance campaign that tried to call for quicker diagnosis of people with Cancer and more consistent modes of treatment for patients across the UK. She wanted people to know about 'Headsmart' who have a website and leaflet. They give details about the symptoms of brain tumours and what to do when one is suspected. Natalie's aim was to help parents to recognise the symptoms and to help doctors diagnose babies, children and teenagers with brain tumours much sooner. After Natalie's case, we were pleased to learn that the doctor's surgery where she was first treated began using the leaflet. Natalie did not want to be pitied but was keen to share her story to stop other people going through what she had gone through.

After completing her radiotherapy treatment, her motto was: 'Work hard and party harder.' She worked every shift she could to earn as much money she could for her holidays and the nice things she liked. She was disappointed, though, that she was never seizure-free and to be able to sit her driving test, but she did not dwell on it. The Teenage Cancer Trust sent her on a few of their outings, including the yearly conference 'Where's Your Sense of Tumour.' We were able to watch her at one of the events on YouTube, wearing a silly 'See you Jimmy hat', dancing and singing 'Donald Where's Your Trousers.' She kept pulling up her leggings in the clip and when I talked about the footage with her through a medium it surprised me when she said: "I was fat there, Mum." I laughed as she was concerned about how she looked even when she was in the afterlife.

Natalie went out partying with her family and friends in Stirling, then came up to visit me and have a relaxing time at the beach. She chilled, playing with her little

could. I was taken to the boot of a car to be shown what had been bought for her. When the car boot opened, the sight of a wheelchair knocked me sideways. Floods of tears escaped from my eyes as it was a clear sign her abilities were dwindling and her life slowly ebbing away.

I was at home again with my son Cameron when I got word that Natalie would need intravenous chemo. I packed my bags and made my way down to stay with her in hospital while she had the treatment. When I arrived to take her to hospital, I realised how disabled she was becoming, but I did not fully understand how much the tumour was consuming her. At first, she had been dragging her foot only slightly in October, then I had to hold on to her as she slid and nearly fell over when I helped her move from a hospital bed to a commode by March. Reality hit me of what was to come. For two years, Natalie had been skipping around and past the deep pull of the world of Cancer. As she lay in the hospital bed, I could see it was engulfing her and fast. We looked at the bag of magic potion being fed into her veins with great hope and renewed enthusiasm.

A view-point of life I would rather not have experienced was to witness a hospital ward where expelled hair was common-place. Natalie knew her beloved hair was going to start falling out. Oh, how she loved her hair; she loved nothing more about herself. We went to the hospital beauty department as we had an appointment for us both to have our hair cut. The build-up to it was fun. Natalie wanted to go first; she got a short style as it was put to her she would notice losing her hair less if it was short. Cutting her hair short must have felt like a great loss to her as her long blonde hair was what she liked best about herself. I had grown my hair purposely down to my waist, longer than usual for this very day – a day I hoped in my heart would not come - not because I was losing my hair but because I understood that in time, I could potentially lose my daughter. The volunteer hairdresser had his hands poised and he looked at me: "Are you sure?" I gave a quick nod of my head and with hardly much thought or time to back down, the electric clippers shaved off my long curly hair.

I felt joy about donating my hair to the Little Princess Trust that makes wigs for children who are fighting Cancer or have other illnesses. Natalie was given a real hair wig which was styled and cut in readiness for her to use, but she became very ill so fast and never got to wear it. Looking back on it, I had the best laugh and an overwhelming feeling of tremendous love while sharing that moment in time, that wonderful experience with my daughter when we both lost our hair. When my head was bald she kept saying: "Wow, Wow!" The laughter was priceless. I hold that memory deep in my heart.

I was given the relatives' room to sleep in when Natalie was having her treatment. It did not click then, but I was told these rooms were only given to relatives of people who were dying. I believed I was only staying there because Natalie needed help with most basic things. She was becoming severely disabled down the right side of her body due to a tumour in her left side and now in another place deep in the middle of her brain. I naively thought her disabilities would improve when her tumour was eradicated. While staying in the relatives' room, I woke through the night due to the extreme cold from having an uncovered head so I made my way back to Natalie's bedside. As I was on my way to her room, I experienced the friendly nods of the head and silent hellos from fellow patients and relatives who may have thought I was fighting Cancer with my shaved head. I explained to one woman that I was there with my daughter, supporting her. I don't know why I felt the need to explain myself to a stranger. She congratulated me on my efforts, but instead of feeling as if I had cleared up a pre-conceived thought, it just made me feel worse. It was one of those many moments when I asked myself: *why did I say that*? I stayed beside Natalie for the rest of her stay in hospital. After a few days in hospital, Natalie returned home to her dad's house where we waited for the chemo to start bringing her back to us.

She had an appointment at the hospital after being given her intravenous chemotherapy to discuss her progress. My mum and I sat in shock as a Palliative Nurse introduced herself. The main word I heard in the consultation was 'Palliative' -to me this meant failing to fight the Cancer, the beginning of the end. Natalie had never wanted to know about anything bad, but she plucked up the courage to ask about her disabilities. She was distraught to learn that she would never regain the use of the right side of her body. She cried uncontrollably when she realised her wheel-chair was to stay. I am guessing Natalie's Teenage Cancer nurse had an idea of her chances of survival as she took us into a room and broached the subject:
"Sometimes we can be prepared if we know." Natalie did not want her to continue the conversation any further; she did not want to know if there was a possibility she would die or when it might happen. I am guessing the specialist knew at this point where Natalie's condition might be heading.

It was not long before we were back in hospital for Natalie's second lot of intravenous chemotherapy. The Teenage Cancer Trust ordered Natalie a large pizza for her lunch and showed her a room where she could go to watch films and play computer games. She watched a little of a film with me while we cuddled on her bed, but she felt too tired to bother with the pizza and was not well enough to go to the teenage room. I looked at her mobile phone on her bedside table next to her. It rang and binged notifying her of all her friends trying to contact to her, but she didn't even look at it. This was so unlike her – she lived for her phone and her chats with her friends. Watching her drift away from her phone was the first time I felt the void that comes from grief begin to open up. Natalie had been getting visual disturbances in her right eye and as she chatted to the junior doctor who was checking her over, she told him she could only see a bright white light in it. The doctor smiled and got off his chair and left the room without asking any more questions. I took Natalie outside in her wheelchair around the grounds of the hospital for some fresh air, then came back to find her Teenage Cancer nurse waiting to chat to her.

I settled Natalie back into the room shortly before a few doctors, Natalie's Teenage Cancer nurse and other staff we didn't know came in and sat around us. The consultant looked at Natalie in a sympathetic manner, asking her various questions about her condition. The words "the chemotherapy is not working" will ring in my ears for ever more. There was no point in her having any further doses of intravenous chemotherapy as it was not helping her to fight the Cancer. I naively thought that, perhaps, she could have radiotherapy as that had worked before. I was told she could only have radiotherapy once as further treatment would not have any effect on her tumour. The consultant finished his meeting with us by saying he would go and discuss her case with the other specialists and left us with a slither of hope. When they left the room, Natalie and I sat as if we had been stranded on a highway and our bus ride had pulled away without us. I was confused and was left to wonder what just happened there. There was a brief discussion about another type of tablet which may help her, but the results from that drug could be negligible.

I phoned Natalie's family and had to tell them the news over the phone and asked them to make their way to the hospital. I called my mum and made sure someone was with her while I slowly gave her the grave news. I heard my mum collapse in shock as Bert and my mum's friend Jenny held her. The oncologist came back with Natalie's Teenage Cancer nurse and the Palliative Care nurse and sat by Natalie's bed. I was sitting beside Natalie, embracing her as we listened intensively to what they had to say. I found it hard to concentrate on the doctor's words due to the emotional pain consuming my whole being. Forever tears were flowing from us all as they told us Natalie could go home with no more needles, no more treatment as there was no more they could do for her. For the first time throughout her journey, Natalie asked the question. She was told she probably had "Weeks to months" to live. I stared at the consultant in disbelief. How had this happened? Natalie had been full of life such a short time ago. I will always be amazed at my daughter who seemed to take the news with such bravery. She put me to shame in my state of grief. The team of staff left the room quietly. As we hugged Natalie and tried to come to terms with the thought of losing her, she turned to us and said: "Keep it Happy."

When a labouring woman comes under my care I have an idea what may happen to her in relation to her situation, but sometimes we just don't know. I wondered if the specialists looking after Natalie had a kind of knowledge like that about her situation, the kind of knowledge which is best kept under a hat until it needs to be shared. When Natalie was deciding whether to have radiotherapy or chemotherapy, the consultant told me no matter what, Natalie's life would be shortened considerably. When asked, he gave me an estimation of her being able to live 'Possibly five to thirty years.' As I said, sometimes we just don't know. I heard the number thirty, but Natalie only got two.

While I lay in her dad's spare room adjacent to Natalie's room, I could hear sobbing through the night. I desperately wanted to go to her to see if she needed me, but I was not in my own home and I had no idea if it was her who was crying or someone else. The tumour was gripping her more and more day by day, and she slept more deeply and longer as time went on so I did not want to disturb her. I thought if it was her, perhaps she needed space to express her emotions. When she wanted me near her, I sat or lay beside her on her bed while we chatted like old times. During these precious times, I began trying to coach her on her journey to the after-life. I was glad she had a belief in something other than 'when you die that is it', as it gave her hope in a different way. I told her that when her time came, she was to let go and fly as high as she could and as fast as she could and not look back. We hugged and cried hysterically together, but we could not hide from or dance around the subject of death anymore.

Natalie's family got upset with me for distressing her, so I drove home away from my girl to give them all space. I broke my heart the whole four hours of that car journey, wailing uncontrollably while I had the privacy to express my pain. Natalie's family phoned me the next day to say Natalie wanted her mum back, so I packed my bags and took my mum down with me to move into her house to be with her till the end.

It was heartbreaking to see my girl deteriorate infront of my eyes. She tried to tell me she wanted the blinds down on the window to stop the sun hurting her eyes but could not find the words: "Sky down," she said. I couldn't help her, it felt wrong to watch her get more poorly and not be able to take her to a doctor to get better. No matter what happened, there was nothing else that could be done. She was given an electric chair which manoeuvred so she could get in and out of it easily. She broke her heart the day she could no longer climb the stairs of the house to get to her bedroom. A hospital bed arrived in the downstairs spare room, a sure sign of what lay ahead of us. She began sleeping a lot more on her hospital bed. Some days she didn't want to do much, but other days she was wide awake as if it was all a joke.

During one of her wide-awake periods, she got out of bed and dragged herself to the toilet. We asked her if she wanted to do anything that day. Before we knew it, she was in my car and ready for an outing, apparently to go and get ice-cream. Natalie, my mum, Colin and I were huddled in my car driving around the Hillfoots of Stirling. Natalie always loved to look her best as she took great pride in her appearance. The drugs, mostly the steroids, had made her gain weight at an alarming rate, more quickly than she had time to get used to it. Previously, she had painstakingly got back down to her normal weight after her last lot of treatment. This must have been so upsetting for her, but she didn't let it show. However, on this special outing she suddenly changed her mind about going for an ice-cream. I caught her looking around and thought she either did not like the thought of people watching her eating ice-cream or she genuinely became tired all of a sudden and wanted to go home there and then. We had on occasions taken ice-cream home to have after dinner, but for some reason she did not want to do this either.

As days went by, Natalie's awake and energetic periods were becoming less and less, so these periods were precious and had to be snapped up and enjoyed. We tried to make good memories as best as we could. I could see our time with her was near running out. The last outing my mum and I had with Natalie was to take her to the grounds of the University of Stirling. It is a nature reserve so it is quite beautiful, especially on a sunny day. I sat and watched my daughter soaking up the moment. I reminisced about the times I spent there while doing my midwifery training and all the other times I had taken my children there for walks. I shifted my thoughts back to Natalie, wondering what she must be feeling. I tried to enjoy the heat of the sun while I watched in amazement at how the water was sparkling with what looked like twinkling stars bouncing along the water from the blinding glare of the sun. It was a sight which seemed unearthly, almost magical, as if some other force was creating this amazing sight. I was witnessing something so loving and beautiful with one of the loves of my life. Time stood still, allowing an unusual stillness and quietness to envelope us. The serenity was complemented by the flapping of birds' wings and their playful commotion on the water. The grass was lushgreen, the trees had many colours and the pretty blooming flowers glowed in the sun. I wanted the experience to last forever, partly so Natalie could enjoy it as much as possible but mostly so I could always have her by my side. My mum broke the golden silence with a question which felt like an unwanted intrusion. I answered my mum's question but remained wondering how we could be experiencing something so beautiful at a time of such great sorrow.

I watched my daughter sitting in her wheelchair which she hardly had time to become accustomed to and wondered what was going through her mind. I felt an indescribable pain for her. Her life had changed so quickly. She had to deal with so much loss. Such loss must have been hard to endure with her being so dependent while being at the optimum age when her life should be taking off. I will always wonder how she coped with that. I deeply wanted to cry, but this was a precious time to be savoured and remembered - to cry would have spoiled the moment and upset Natalie. I blocked these tears as best I could for the rest of her journey of passing over so I could help her gain the strength and courage to leave us and go to an unknown realm. I switched my focus onto her and how I could help her 'Keep it Happy.' I cuddled her and asked: "If the sky was the limit and you could do anything you wanted, what would it be?" "I'd like to go to Hawaii, like that's going to happen?" "Okay," I said. "What is it about Hawaii that you want to go there?" Her answer was swift and simple: "The sea!" I knew she loved to be at the seaside so we put the wheels in motion to get her to see the sea for one last time.

I sold my house and bought one near Natalie's house with a downstairs bedroom and toilet with Natalie's disabilities in mind. This was shortly before I knew she was going to die so she only got to see it from outside. I began moving into my new home while family members took Natalie to The Malcolm Sargent House in Prestwick, which is on the seafront. It took great effort, but Natalie managed to enjoy an ice-cream while having a fantastic view of the sea. This was difficult for her as she was deteriorating at a faster speed than before. She spent most of her time at this house sleeping but still managed to grab happy moments.

I got a phone call while I was moving furniture into my new home to say Natalie wanted me to join them on her holiday. When my mum and I arrived at The Malcolm Sargent House, I couldn't stop the tears escaping from my eyes. The sight of my daughter with her head falling to her right side while she was being fed her dinner was too much for me to take. For the first time, she looked as if she had severe brain damage. A simpler form of Natalie sat before me. This anguish was transferred to a huge feeling of love as she gave me the biggest smile ever, showing me how happy she was to have me with her. It was so typical of Natalie – she would not miss out on a holiday even when she was really too ill to be there.

When Natalie slept at night, I slept beside her. She would shout 'Mum' and I would go to her and help her with her every need. We used a baby alarm to hear her calling out to us when she was awake. When she slept during the day, my mum and close relatives sat in the day room, and on one occasion we discussed her funeral arrangements. I found it too painful to think too much about her leaving us or plan her funeral, but I understood it was the best way to fulfil Natalie's wishes for saying goodbye.

I realised how ill Natalie was becoming; it had been a struggle to take her on holiday so I broached the subject with the rest of the family. "If we wait too long we may not be able to get her home." The Malcolm Sargent House staff allowed us to take Natalie home using their minibus. We held our breath as we struggled to get her into the minibus to make the journey home. A family member sat at either side of her, holding her. I drove my car at the back of the minibus, willing our girl to get home. We all hugged and cried when we managed to get her safely into her hospital bed. Natalie cried in the minibus. We guessed it was because she knew she was going home to die. We wanted to give The Malcolm Sargent House a sum of money for their funds as a huge 'thank you', but they told us they could not accept it. We had to give it to the charity organisation rather than to the House directly. It upset me to learn this House is now closed due to lack of funds.

When Natalie got home, she melted into her bed as much as the Cancer melted into her. She slept more than she was awake. We had to take her to the fridge in the kitchen in her wheelchair to see what she wanted to eat, because she had lost the words for her favourite food. We all had fun with her as we occasionally pinched some sweets out of her large tub of goodies she had beside her. Eventually, her sweetie tub remained untouched and she didn't want to go and pick anything to eat. Her body was giving up. We bought her a bell to ring when her words faded away. Family and friends gave her presents she could neither eat nor look at. I wondered how they could not understand how ill she was but in saying that, Natalie only allowed her close friends and her close family group of carers to see her the way she was. We fulfilled her three wishes of not letting people see her near the end, taking her to see the sea for the last time and help her die at home.

The Macmillan nurses appeared with a box full of medication and leaflets on what to expect when a loved one dies. They started the ball rolling on how to help Natalie on her final journey. Music played constantly, and we all took turns to be with her. We all said our private goodbyes, then gave her space to sleep when she wanted to. Eventually, her body lay in the room, but her mind appeared to have drifted away. She struggled with her breathing so the family gathered around at eight o' clock in the evening. We sat her upright so she could breathe, then lay her down again when she fell back asleep. Realising how settled and comfortable she had become, the family dispersed but remained close by.

A Marie Curie volunteer nurse came to give us some rest through the night, but I found it hard to settle. It had been my wish and my responsibility in Natalie's family group of carers to keep a night vigil beside her bed for many weeks. She would shout "Mum!" when she needed me. 'Mum' being a solitary word her scrambled mind had managed to hold onto up until then. All modes of communication had gone. It was as if she had already stepped into the next world and was holding onto this world by her fingertips. I eventually gave into exhaustion and lay down on the couch for a short while. The Marie Curie nurse woke me to tell me Natalie was struggling with her breathing once more. The sight of her struggling to catch a breath caused me great heart ache. My baby was distressed and there was very little I could do about it.

We called for the on-call practice nurse to attend. As soon as she arrived, I begged her to give Natalie more morphine. The practice nurse tried to explain that she had to be very careful not be seen to be the one who caused Natalie's death. How ironic? Natalie was already dying with such struggle. What had the world come to, to allow people to suffer this way? The anguish of watching my daughter fight to breathe and seeing her in pain was too much for me. My family had successfully deterred me from giving her morphine before the on-call nurse arrived. I had been pushed to the brink and thought *'to hang' with the consequences*! I was linked with her, crying the tears she could not shed, her pain was my pain. Eventually, the practice nurse realised that Natalie did need more pain relief. After the morphine top-up was given, Natalie slipped into a deeper sleep while I settled down to hold her hand once more.

Nurses from a local Hospice called 'Strathcarron Hospice at Home' helped us with Natalie's personal hygiene. They arrived cheerily as they had done every day for a week or two, but on realising their time with Natalie was done, gave us a swift sympathetic hug and left. This was a loving embrace which was an acknowledgement of our pain, a hug that brought the realisation: "This is it" and started a lifetime of tears from grief.

Every time Natalie drifted into a deep sleep she fought herself awake, trying to hold on as long as she could. It took another top-up of morphine from an on-call doctor before she relaxed and stopped fighting. I stared at her young face, trying to capture every detail of her in my mind, then the sight of her foot caught my eye. It lay uncovered and unprotected. It looked so tiny, so normal, so Natalie, unlike the rest of her body which had been taken over by the Cancer. I thought *there are no shoes in the world that can protect her now*. As soon as we gave our girl permission to let go and find peace she gave in to her fate. Six weeks after Natalie was told her life would end she slipped away with her family all around her. We looked at each other's wet faces and smiled a knowing smile when the television switched itself off shortly after she left our world.

BEGINING TO FEEL THE LOVE

Riding the Waves

They say questioning the beginning and the meaning of life can be provoked by the process of grieving when we have been touched by death, an ending. The beginning of the end of my daughter's life remains unclear. We will never know when the essence of her brain tumour first appeared. Experts say it was probably present most, if not all of her life. Was the tumour in the making before she was even born? Was it indirectly caused by the cocktail of drugs her dad was given by the Armed Forces in preparation for him to defend our country in the Gulf War? Was it a result of her falling off her bike head first when she was six years old or when she was thrown off a horse head first when she was having a riding lesson at eleven years old? If it was there all her life, was it triggered into growing rapidly by a blow to her head by a drunk and upset friend or could it have stemmed from the time someone accidentally banged her head against a wall in a stair corridor? I am the only person out of five female family members who has not had Cancer. I am also the only one who has never drunk coffee or smoked cigarettes. Could there be a common link or a trigger for the high rate of Cancer in my family due to the substances ingested from food or beverages or inhaled from cigarettes? I often wonder if I have been spared the disease so far due to opening my third-eye and working with healing energy.

No matter what the cause was, the guilt of not being able to protect my daughter from brain cancer will always haunt me. Sometimes, I wish I had given her pure cannabis oil to see if it would have helped her. I guess this is part of the grieving process: the blaming, anger, frustration and reflection, agonising over the 'what if, wish I had, wish they had' or 'we all should have.'

My resolution came in the guise of an unearthly concept. Natalie was able to relay, no matter what happened, that she was always going to die young. She had a short contract for this life and was going to die early as part of her pre-ordained path. She had fulfilled what she had planned to do on earth and it was her time to go. No matter how many times a parent is told it was meant to be, the loss can never be justified or accepted as it is not deemed normal for parents to outlive their children.

The sympathy cards came in thick and fast. Each one a knock on my head, bringing me out of my dazed state to remind me – yes, she was gone. I appreciated the love people were trying to send me, but I did not want to see the physical proof of her death. I hid the cards without reading them. Phone calls came asking me how I was. I did not know how to answer this question. I had no idea how I was. At times I felt crazy – from the early days to two years after Natalie's funeral.

The weeks following my daughter's death had me living outside of my skin. I experienced a form of amnesia, which – I guess – was due to taking harmful prescription drugs and alcohol. I excused my behaviour by having the rationale of trying to cure the insomnia and numb the pain which raced through my veins every hour of day and night. My emotions built up like hot lava in a volcano which was up to boiling point and ready to erupt. I began to write notes about what happened to Natalie and all the emotions I was riding through. Writing out word after word seemed to help ooze out the deep pain in my heart and gave my eyes permission to release tear after tear.

I thought about other people who were going through what Natalie had been through and felt a magnetic pull to help them. I was well aware that I was finding a way to get through each day with a purpose, but it could otherwise be seen as a form of denial and avoidance of my grief. I had no idea what I was doing from day to day, never mind think about what we would plan or achieve in the year following Natalie's death.

My cousin Janice set up a giving page for us to raise funds for The Teenage Cancer Trust. Janice successfully ran a race on the day of Natalie's funeral. All the funds from Natalie's funeral, donations of support from our family, friends, neighbours and work colleagues were added to the page. This was the beginning of our Team effort in fund-raising for a few Cancer-related charities in Natalie's name.

Nurses from Strathcarron Hospice at Home helped us fulfil Natalie's wish of staying at home till the end. I watched them chat to her as they gently washed her immobile body. With tear-filled eyes, I asked them how I could ever repay them. They gave us support in more ways than they may have realised. Then I had an idea. When Natalie was born on Hogmanay in 1994, we remarked how special her twenty-first birthday party would be. This was a party not destined to happen as she died just after she turned twenty years old. I planned to mark what would have been her big birthday by having a party to raise money for the Hospice funds. I called it our 'Highland Fling' as I saw it as our last Highland fling together. I taught Natalie Highland dancing and we used to go to a dancing class together when she was young.

Natalie's family and friends worked together to make the event run smoothly and raise a good amount of money. I painted a large picture of Olaf and cut out carrot noses. The children filled the room with laughter as they hunted for the noses to pin on Olaf. One of Natalie's friends dressed up in an Olaf costume which was donated by Central Mascots Company in Stirling. I spent many months contacting local businesses asking for donations for our raffle so we had a huge list of prizes. My mum and family members organised the big draw at the charity event. My son, Colin, organised a Guess the Baby Doll's Birthday competition. My aunt Lily organised the Tombola and also made the invitations with my uncle Andrew. Family and friends brought food and Greggs the baker shop where Natalie had worked also supplied food and a large cake. My mum organised the buffet while Bert and my uncle Andrew chatted over their beer as they sold tickets at the door. My husband Andy spent most of the day filling numerous balloons with helium his former boss at BOC had donated. He attached 'Post Cards to Heaven' to each one.

'Post Cards to Heaven' were postcards I designed for people to buy and write a message for their lost loved ones. My mother-in-law Maureen and her friends sold a great number of postcards which were released at the bells in many Bowling clubs throughout the Central Belt. We released our balloons and postcards at quarter past six in the evening as this was the time of Natalie's birth. It would have been the moment she was a woman in this world. In my mind, she stepped into the afterlife as a child but with this milestone became a fully-grown independent individual no matter where she was. She reassured me she would be with us when we were having the event, but I was so busy organising the children's entertainment I never stopped to feel her around me until the end. As I watched the balloons colour the sky, it seemed as if the immense surge of love in our letters enabled our two worlds to merge, as if I could almost touch her.

Our event was successful in bringing us all together on such a special day and it provided the biggest avoidance I could think of. The postcards were decorated with a rainbow around my poem and the stamp was a picture of my favourite photo of Natalie doing a 'Thumbs up' pose.

Postcard to Heaven

I wish I could fly like white doves in the sky
or climb over rainbows to reach you up high.
I miss you each day that we are apart
so I am sending this message straight from my heart.
My love for you will never wane.
I will keep it safe till we meet again.

HEAVENLY MESSAGE

Natalie's friends set up Just-Giving pages for Cancer-related charities. Shannon did a Charity run and Gemma did a sky dive as Natalie had always wanted to do one. I advised Natalie a sky dive may not be the best thing for her to do when she had just undergone surgery and six weeks intensive radiotherapy on her brain. Family members did the Brave Shave and other running events. My mum and Maureen raised funds with whiskey competitions with Ann, Bob and Jean. My mum, Lily and Andrew helped me run a stall for charity where I offered alternative therapies and sold cakes and tablet. My best friend Babs, who is Natalie's Godmother, held a Sponsored Hack. Natalie used to go riding with Babs and took weekly lessons on Solo, a horse Babs owns. Four-year-old Cameron proudly led the long procession around a designated route on Solo. Babs and her friends and family all came together with their horses to make the day fun and a success. It is not uncommon for people like us who have lost a loved one to hold events to raise funds for charity. Some inspiring people have the strength and enthusiasm to make it a lifetime quest.

Four months after Natalie died, I received a phone call from the staff at Strathcarron Hospice at Home to ask me if I would like to help them by telling my story on television. They wanted to try and win the National Lottery Award to raise money for their funds, but mostly to create a bigger awareness of the work they do. I went to the Hospice where the staff and I were interviewed by reporters from the Stirling Observer, the Daily Record and Central Radio Station. I talked about how the nurses helped us carry out Natalie's wish to die at home and asked people to vote for them.

Once the votes had been counted, I received a phone call from a television producer called Annie. She asked me to go to the Hospice with family members and friends to tell our story on television. My mum, Colin and Natalie's best friend Gemma came with me. My mum refused to go on camera so Colin, Gemma and I were recorded for some time before they told us it was a wrap. Half-way through the day, the producer advised me time was short so my clip would be the only one they would be using. I wondered why they were focusing on me as Colin and Gemma were young, articulate and pleasing to the eye so would make good subjects for the show. I had gained a lot of weight while grieving, had short unmanageable hair after having it shaved off and did not have time to go shopping for a new outfit for the recording. I was aware that I was looking the worst I had ever looked in my life while sitting in-front of the camera. My ambition of helping the nurses to do their work spurred me on to let the tears flow as I spoke about my girl.

Some time later, I was asked to sit in the tea room at Strathcarron Hospice to talk to the nurses and managers. I was chatting and enjoying their company when Anton du Beke, who starred in the Strictly Come Dancing show, came into the room. I had no idea why he was there and what all the fuss was about. The mystery was solved when he announced that Strathcarron Hospice at Home had won the National Lottery Award. I felt elated; the embarrassment of showing myself as I was in the media and all the emotions I had to endure when talking about my girl had been worthwhile. Our efforts had been successful in helping the Hospice do the work they do for people like Natalie. The nurses and managers had a fabulous and well-deserved night out in London when they were filmed receiving their award. The show was televised on Lottery Stars 2015 and can still be seen online. The Hospice has helped and continues to help many people so it was no surprise to hear they were overrun with votes to win. Due to this, the Hospice has been given further help from the Lottery Fund for the next few years.

During a break in the filming, I was able to have idle chatter and a wee sing-song with Anton. When the work was complete, Anton was filmed dancing with the staff. This was an unexpected clip they televised. After Anton danced with me he stood back in surprise: "You can dance!" I guess the television crew did not run the clip of me dancing salsa with him as it probably was not deemed appropriate for a grieving mother to be seen dancing. Some of the crew joked about how I could be put on the Strictly Come Dancing show as a red herring one day. I knew I did not have the looks or a trim body to be on the show, but for politeness's sake I replied: "With pleasure." Before Anton left, he took time to meet my mum, Colin and Gemma. My mum and Gemma were overcome with excitement as they idolised him, so he posed for a photo with us before being on his way.

The two schools Natalie had attended organised charity days. Bannockburn Primary School held a Dress-Down Day and Bannockburn High School held a Wear-aTouch-of-Purple Day. Children from both schools were pictured with us giving Strathcarron Hospice at Home their cheque in memory of Natalie. The story was again highlighted in the local paper. During the week Bannockburn High School held their charity day, I noticed Anton du Beck was dancing on television wearing a touch of purple on his dance outfit. I would like to believe he was showing us his support in his own private way.

I thought of many ways I could make money to raise funds for charity. One of these ideas included asking people if they would write a poem about their experience of separation and loss. I planned to collate the poems to produce a book to sell for charity and help other grieving people, but I received too few to complete this task. The emotions of life can be very personal and upsetting and it can be difficult to write about them, never mind share them. One individual took the time to put a negative into a positive by writing a poem for me. They had the courage to share their feelings about the loss of their loved one and their confusion of finding themselves on the wrong road in life following their loss. I wanted to use their poem so their effort would not be in vain. I hope Angels like my dad are with this person, showing them the way back. Perhaps, they find comfort in seeing their words being shared to help others.

Prayer to an Angel

Since the day you were taken
to be with the Angels in the sky,
my heart has been so heavy
and all I do is cry,
because there were so many things
I would have loved to say and do.
which would just involve me and you.

I miss and love you
from the bottom of my heart.
But listen princess, it's just the start.
Because someone's go to do it,
the whole things out of hand.
Why it's got to this stage,
I will never understand.

I miss you, I love you.
My mind is in a muddle.
The only thing I need most from you,
believe me, is a cuddle.

Anon.

Feeling the Pain

When trying to cope with separation and loss, we can gather ourselves and soar like an eagle, grabbing opportunities which come our way or plummet to the deepest depths of darkness and lock ourselves away indefinitely. I became exhausted with the lack of sleep, working, looking after my son and trying to help others. I switched my focus on how I could help myself but found there were limited resources and help out there for me. Some people like me feel the need to search out psychic people who can help us by contacting our loved ones in the spirit world.

I am aware there are some so-called fake mediums around who could cause damage to people who are already suffering. I was lucky to find a kind, gifted and sensitive medium. Mediums and spiritualists focus on helping us link with our loved ones in the afterlife so we can be given reassurance and guidance. Fortune-tellers usually focus on predicting our future, but we are the controller. We have free will to change our direction in life at any given time so our future is not usually set in stone. This may be why anyone with foresight can be viewed as fake or not accurate.

Most sensitive people get messages from spirit for other people, but rarely are they given messages for themselves. I am no different. I realised through a medium in Inverness that there are some things which can't be fully explained at our level of being. Natalie and I visited her before Natalie was diagnosed with her illness. I could not understand why spirit and none of the mediums I knew could tell me what was wrong with my daughter. I realise now that if Natalie did not want spirit to tell her about her illness or tell her she was going to die then it was not my place to know either. I have to accept that there are times spirit does not send me messages or warnings to help prevent bad things happening around me. I can only act on the messages they do send.

Sometimes, sensitive people can feel spirit around them without messages being relayed. I could feel Natalie near me so felt the compelling urge to request further contact with her through my spiritual adviser, Patsy. My low mood meant my vibrations were low and dense, making it impossible for my daughter to reach me. Was I leaning on her memory too much, not allowing her to fly and be free from the constraints of my misery? I jolted myself upright. It was not in my nature to hem my sons and daughter in. I wanted them to live life to the full and be free to follow their hearts. To hang on to Natalie so tightly in an emotional or energetic sense hit me as being unfair and uncharacteristic of me. It was time for me to listen to my own teaching and loosen the ropes. I needed to take responsibility for my own state of health while still loving my girl more than ever.

Patsy confirmed that Natalie was back around me as I was still sad and needed to be uplifted. Natalie laughed about how I made myself touch her body in her coffin. I wanted to be the last to touch her and say 'goodbye' as I was the first to feel her inside me. I was the one who felt her come into the world and the one who felt her go. She reassured me that she was fine and said she would walk with me while I found my way back to life through my writing. When I sensed her energy around me, it gave me a lift to look at the sun, even though I could not feel it.

I had to find my own way back and in my own time. Some people seem to get through the journey of grief quickly, while others go around in circles before they can find their way out to see the brightness again. There were occasions when I thought I was getting better, and then another wave would hit me without warning. It felt similar to trying to drive a car from the back seat, not quite reaching the pedals to stop and not being able to turn the wheel to go where I wanted to go. I preferred my head in the sand, soaked with alcohol, because the emotions I was riding were too much for my broken heart. When I talked to other people about my grief, I learned that some of them were still suffering years after the loss of their loved ones, unable to let go. I was like a salmon fish fighting to swim up-river, trying to get back to my roots, to get back to me. I did not realise I needed to find and accept a new me.

Natalie was right when she told me that I had stopped doing the things I love. I wondered: *When did I lose my fight for life, where was the light within me now*? I had been living for Cameron, but eventually this was not enough. My daughter's presence was the only thing which could reassure and comfort me. I realised that for some of us, the knowledge of an afterlife existing where our loved ones live on can cause the spark which ignites us to start living life again. I am a firm believer in the existence of an afterlife due to the contact I have had with Natalie and other loved ones who have died. The spiritual interventions I have had in my life and having the ability to feel the healing energy I work with fortify this belief.

A tiny thought of my daughter could make tears push through my stiff upper lip at any time without warning. When I had good days, I felt so in-touch with Spirit and could feel Natalie with me. I could feel Spirit filling me with energy, propping me up, making me feel taller than the trees and wider than the horizons. Our entwined energy made me feel as if I could reach every soul in the world. It felt strange to feel so disconnected with life and then connected to every living thing on earth and beyond.

Having a little knowledge about the afterlife was worse than having no knowledge at all. I desperately needed to understand more, mostly about where my daughter was. Patsy told me Natalie was a young soul when she passed but was also a strong spirit with a deep connection to me and other members of her family. Natalie let me know she was aware of the sore heads I was having and was massaging my forehead at night while I was in bed. I taught her when she was young how to do this. She said my house was too quiet and reminded me that I used to sing and dance around the house when I played music. "Put the music on, Mum," she said. Then she changed the subject by saying she loved going on 'our walks.' She was talking about the daily walks I take Harvey on. She used to smother our waggy-tailed cocker spaniel dog with love. She was the only person who could make him roll over with the promise of a biscuit for his trick. She confirmed she had been leaving signs everywhere to let us know she was still around us. Patsy paused in the reading to tell me Natalie was making the lights in her room flicker. I laughed as Natalie was making my lights flicker at the same time just as she had done many times before that day. Some of us believe flickering lights can be Spirit's way of trying to communicate with us; sometimes they use Morse code.

Little feathers and pennies appeared at my feet indoors and outdoors. It happened regularly when I sat in parks watching Cameron play with other children. One occasion in particular had me perplexed. I put my mobile phone down on my coffee table, turned away and when I turned back there was a one-pence coin sitting on the magnetic part of the flip-closure of my phone. On another day, I was sitting in a taxi cab quite sad in the midst of a difficult day, until a one-pence coin appeared on the seat to my right side. It was not there when I had climbed into the taxi. When I commented on the penny, the driver insisted I give him the coin. He tapped it to his forehead and thanked unseen forces for the gift. A little euro the same size of a penny and a white feather appeared at my feet when I was on holiday in the Algarve. There were no feathered furnishings in that apartment so I understood it as being Natalie's way of saying she would not miss out on a holiday. She told me before she died she would try and contact me if she could. She could always turn it up a notch when she was alive and began doing this when she started sending me twenty-pence coins everywhere until I had no doubt it was her sending them to me.

She told me to watch out for a bird coming close to me. True to her word, while I was frantically writing my book in my garden, a little bird hung around me for days. I often sat quietly in my garden, deep in my thoughts. On one of these occasions a monarch butterfly came down and rested for a prolonged time on the table next to me. I took a photo of it and then watched it in wonderment. I was given confirmation that it was, indeed, Natalie manipulating the butterfly so I would know she was still around. When she was young, I told her the spirit of a loved one is usually close to us when a butterfly comes near.

It is possible for those in the afterlife to be able to manipulate energy, like kinetic energy, which can hide or move objects around. Colin didn't believe me when I told him some of my things were going missing. We laughed when we discovered I was not going mad. During a psychic reading my Great-Gran told me she had been hiding objects from me to demonstrate how she can manipulate the energy around them.

In response to Natalie sending me Heavenly Messages of feathers, pennies, butterflies, birds, flickering lights and certain songs on the radio, I was inspired to write a poem to try and capture the everlasting love I felt was still present between us and the emotions running through me after losing her so young.

Heavenly Message

Here I am, yet another long night
filled with memories good and bad.
I close my eyes to see you
and remember all the times we had.

I looked down at you and saw the future,
it brought a smile to my face.
I held you close to bring comfort
and sensed the wonder of God's grace.

You blossomed in your teenage years
with great beauty, wisdom and shone bright.
You stole the hearts of many, and stood out
like a shining diamond, so perfect and so right.

Unable to stop the feeling of loneliness,
sadness and the tears.
Can't stop thinking you fought hard, my girl,
then were robbed of many years.

Keep sending the signs that remind me
you are still mine.
They help me ease the pain of separation
and help the passage of time.

Rainbows, white feathers, butterflies
and flying birds at play.
Songs on the radio
and lights flickering away.

All that is real in our two worlds
is the love that we can share.
I can feel your arms around me,
and know you are always there.

HEAVENLY MESSAGE

During a tea-break at work in a maternity unit many years ago, I was in deep conversation with a midwife who was quite a bit older than me who had lost her husband. At the time, I could not understand her logic and thought she was crazy and needed help when she told me she was ready to go. She believed her life was done and would be quite happy to leave this world. It has taken me to lose my daughter to finally understand her and feel exactly the same way. I have found it is not uncommon when you lose a loved one to try and live in their world, trying to keep them close to you while you a have a reluctance to live in this world. When I was using photos of Natalie and talking about her in my letters relating to my fund-raising, I was keeping her human existence alive next to me. I was trying to fabricate logical reasons for her life and death to make her absence mean something. Raising funds can be seen as an unbeatable quest to help block out the pain, the thoughts and feelings which can be overwhelming. When I stepped away from all this work, I began to feel the void opening up at an alarming rate.

I visited the doctor's surgery to ask for something to stop my mind whizzing all over the place. The doctor gave me a quizzical look when I asked: "Do you think I am crazy?" He replied: "The very fact you are asking me that question makes it clear you are not crazy." I hoped the small amount of half-strength sleeping tablets he gave me would stop the burling so I could get snapshots of sleep. Most doctors recommend counselling sessions, but many of these organisations have long waiting lists due to inadequate staffing and funding. I had one half-hour phone consultation with a counsellor, but it did not help; nothing could take away what I was feeling. I felt nothing would work except the passage of time.

They say everyone has a turning point when we change our destructive pattern or our view of life. It may be a time when we are either at our lowest or are in a situation which wakes us from a half-living state. When I was collecting donations for our charity event, I stood in the most plush, expensive-looking hair and beauty salon I had ever seen, with the intention of thanking the Manager for her voucher. It appeared almost too good for a building to be used in this way. Great care had been taken to create lavish surroundings with pretty, well-groomed girls, all busy making polite conversation while they worked. Being from a general working-class background and looking as I did – overweight, draped in my 'bargain snip at the price' second-hand clothing and wild wiry unattended short hair, I felt so out of place and an unwelcome sight in this establishment. As I waited for the manager to appear, I stood embarrassed, jealous at the thought of never being able to have what they have. How I believed these people perceived me and how I was feeling within myself made me want to run.

The Manager entered the room before I had time to leave and gave me a quick glance up and down. She rubbed her nose with her right pointing finger, a distinct motion to me, but probably without her being fully aware of doing it. In those few seconds I realised that if there was a mirror which could show me the total opposite of what I was and what I had become, then this woman was it. This quick negative and displeasing non-verbal sign of the woman in her fancy red dress, shiny long black curly hair and posh demeanour was enough for me to quickly blurt out my reason for being there, hand her my letter and retreat more quickly than the words could reach her ears.

When people noticed my hair not being what it should be, I usually let them know why I looked as I did. On that occasion, it was not something I wanted to explain. I just wanted to get away from the emotions being kicked up in that meeting. I underestimated how much losing my hair would affect the image I had of myself on waking up from a dream state. For some reason, my appearance suddenly mattered as I began wanting to fit in and live in this world, in my physical body.

In contrast, it made me realise how important real hair wigs are to some people who are already going through so much. Giving them a gift of hair can have a huge impact on their self-esteem and ability to overcome the crosses they have to bear. Donating hair is something every female could do without too much trauma to themselves as only eight inches of hair are required to enable the Little Princess Trust to make a wig. The only difficulty I experienced about having my hair shaved off was based on how I could hide my baldness at work. I could not hide the loss of my hair any more than I could hide the pain of loss in my eyes. It was up to me to reach out and seek help to begin healing.

I am no different to the people I have met through my holistic therapy business who have had periods in their lives where they have used harmful substances to achieve a state of absence from life. The trigger for following this path is usually due to difficulties in life which are too hard to accept and overcome. I was part of a team who gave holistic therapies to people who were in a programme to overcome their addictions when I met a lovely lady who enjoyed her massage and healing treatment. I was taken aback when she looked at me and exclaimed: “You have the touch of an Angel.” I have no doubt it was not my hands she was talking about. I am sure she felt the touch of Spirit sending her love and healing through me. Spirit can send us healing and help us with most things in life; all we have to do is ask. They can’t interfere unless we ask them to.

I realised I needed a healing session myself so visited the Spiritual Church during my worst periods. The healers advised me I was out of balance. When we are housed in our physical body we are subjected to many emotions which may become overpowering at times. Grief can shock us into living between worlds to help shield us from the intense emotions. I believe we are subconsciously able to float between our seven body levels or aura energy systems. This is our electromagnetic field which radiates between a centimetre to a meter or more according to our energy levels. Perhaps, this state of euphoria is the kind of existence most people try to reach when they take harmful substances. It is a state where we can live in limbo, hence the saying 'Away with the fairies.' After taking mindaltering substances, it can take around three days for us to come back into our skin and be grounded again. This kind of transition can be achieved without using harmful substances by working with the mind. I wonder if people who suffer from addictions could be helped with training in spiritual meditation, going to spiritual retreats and having healing and alternative therapies.

Using alternative therapies including hypnotherapy and having psychic readings helped me get through the worst stages of my grief. I read books about the afterlife and worked through my thoughts and emotions as I wrote them down. Having the opportunity to contact my daughter in the afterlife was the only thing which helped me begin to accept losing her in my human life. I was aware of slowly returning to my usual self, gaining clarity of mind after I rode through the roughest waves.

Feeling the Love-Link

Natalie advised me through the psychic medium, Diane White, to use the rest of my life to 'feel the love', once I had worked through the worst of my grief. I mistakenly searched for this kind of love in the early part of my life from the men I dated. I was oblivious of how true love was already within me. I just had to open its door to let it shine out and lift me. I thought more about what nourishes and brings the sun out for me – playing music, dancing, reading, painting, my midwifery and healing work - but most of all, I enjoy spending time with my boys.

Cameron has a knack of teaching me how life goes on, as do the responsibilities in my life, whether I want them to or not. Suffering the pain of loss made me think more deeply about myself, my life's purpose and the people and the world around me. I endeavour to put my love back into my work and the people who cross my path. Maintaining a positive way of thinking is important, because I am in contact with many people during my daily work as a midwife.

A midwife is a woman's confidant and ambassador. Upholding a woman's autonomy means midwives can become very close and personal beyond limits normally deemed comfortable or acceptable in most other professions. A bond is usually created quickly and securely between a labouring woman and midwife, a link I am not sure is ever broken. In most cases, women experiencing pregnancy and childbirth need great love and understanding from their midwife and family. Some days are more memorable than others, but most are full of powerful emotions, especially love. Women and their families can experience long harrowing journeys before their baby is placed in their arms, and most have shown great courage while on this journey.

Generally, I am not permitted to speak about women's birth experiences at my work, but one lovely woman knew I was writing my book. She wrote me a letter telling me that she wanted me to add her story to help other people who have been through what she has. Unknown to me initially, she nearly lost her life when she had an Ectopic pregnancy. She suffered the loss of her baby and one of her fallopian tubes. This greatly reduced her chances of becoming pregnant again, so her new baby was a special little soul who came into her life.

She wrote: 'You came in right as I started to push our beautiful baby into the world and said to me: "Right, I want you to show me how much you want this baby." I remember her lying in a sleepy state, totally exhausted and I knew from experience that she was not going to deliver her baby in the state of mind she was in. I did all my tricks to wake her up in readiness for her to meet her baby. She continued: 'Within twenty minutes of you being in the room our gorgeous baby was born. She was born on my late Gran's birthday and then wee things started to happen in the room like machines going off when they weren't on. You said to me: "It's as if someone is here watching over us." This was one delivery when tears swelled up in my eyes while I worked; the love and joy from this baby's mum and dad could have hit the moon and back. I checked their baby over after she was born and placed a purple hat on her head to keep her warm. The little outfit her dad put on her will always stay in my mind and make me smile. It was a white sleep-suit with a picture of a little rainbow. It had the words that read: 'After the storm there is a rainbow of hope .... here I am.' I was thrilled to see a photo of this little rainbow baby and her outfit when I read her mum's story about raising funds for the Ectopic Pregnancy Trust in the Daily Record. This worthwhile cause has so little press – I have known many women who have had an ectopic pregnancy, including my mum. Some have had their chances of having a baby markedly reduced and others have been left unable to have one at all.

Another woman who was lucky enough to have her Rainbow child after an ectopic pregnancy told me how she found out about her pregnancy. She was in her bath with her two-year-old daughter when her daughter pointed at her tummy and said: "Mummy has a baby in her tummy!" "I certainly do not!" was the woman's reply. Two days later, the woman bought a pregnancy test and found her daughter was indeed correct – there was an unplanned but much wanted baby in her tummy.

There is so much love in the world; many people are working hard to help others, but there is also a great deal of the emotion 'fear', which is the nemesis of love. When women are fearful it can cause their labour to slow down or stop altogether, because it depletes their natural production of the hormone oxytocin. This can result in there being a higher risk of women having a traumatic labour and birth experience. A traumatic experience can cause Post-Traumatic-Stress Syndrome. This condition can have a detrimental effect on the lives of women and can interfere with bonding and caring for their baby. I am aware of two occasions where fear has prevented women from coping with their experience and me from being able to reach them to help. I can only reflect on these experiences and find ways around the obstacle of fear. When we talk about 'Fear not' in reality it means we have to try and live life without fear within our own hearts.

On the other hand, fear can be viewed as a positive productive reaction to stimuli as it can cause an effective natural chemical response where adrenaline is produced to enable us to have the resources to escape danger. In the performing arts it is not unusual for people to be nervous and slightly fearful before walking onto a stage. This emotion can give performers an edge to do well in a show. I am sure most of us can recall one or more occasions where fear has helped us in our lives in a difficult or dangerous situation. I can recall a few instances but one event sticks out in my mind more than most.

I was walking with my dog Harvey on a grassy area next to the main road which passes through our town. It was dark and exceptionally cold. I walked many times in this area at night with Harvey for his last walk of the day. I was hunched under many layers of clothing while I crunched over the frozen grass in my Wellington boots. As I approached a dark area where many wild bushes grew, an awful feeling came over me. It was as if someone had put poison in my stomach, as if a high concentration of evil was wrapping around me. My mind was stuck on what could be causing this ill-feeling when Harvey sat down. I beckoned him to continue, but he took two steps forward then sat down again. I was totally freaked out when for the third time he took a step forward and sat down. I realised he must sense the awful feeling, too. I turned around and ran all the way home with Harvey as fast as I could. Just as I reached my house, I slipped on the ice and pulled a muscle on my leg, aggravating a previous injury. I couldn't walk properly so had to stay off work for a couple of weeks. I told my husband I would rather he walked the dog at night.

I thought no more about the incident until it was highlighted on the News a few days later that an elevenyear-old girl had been followed by a man on the local beach not far from where I had been walking on the same day. I did not inform the police as I had not seen anything and thought I may have imagined it all. It is possible either Spirit gave me a warning by enhancing the feeling of fear within me to make me take flight or I actually could feel a vile, evil energy. It was the first and only time I have experienced this awful energy. I sensed it belonged to someone who was visiting the area rather than lived there. I wondered why I had not experienced this energy or feeling when a man had followed me in London. There is a possibility I was more receptive to subtle energy with the incident at that time after I was trained as a Reiki Teaching Master and after mediums from the Stirling Spiritual Church gave me intensive training. Regardless of what it was, I have no doubt Harvey alerted me to something sinister and my adrenaline got me home quickly that night.

Some people deal with traumatic experiences well, but it can be the afterthought which allows distress to creep in. Health Professionals can deal with dire emergencies, using great knowledge and experience with adrenaline giving them an edge to cope. They need time and the opportunity to reflect on these experiences just as much as the women who have been involved in the emergency care. I try to give all women time to reflect after their birth experience, because what I deem normal can be viewed as traumatic by the women and their families.

One lovely lady sent me a letter to thank me for giving her and her husband time to reflect and make light of their experience. She asked if it could be included in my book to help women who may have had a similar experience. She woke up on the morning before her due date with intense contractions. After she helped her children get ready for school, she told her partner she was going to have a bath and get ready to go to hospital. She continues her story: "I stripped off my clothes and was about to step into the bath when suddenly I started to push. Then I started to panic and I shouted for my partner. When he saw me pushing he started running about like a headless chicken. He asked our eldest to accompany the younger ones on the short journey to school. He shoved them all out the front door as he didn't want them to see what was going on. He asked if he should phone an ambulance. I replied: 'Well, aye, obviously!' A lady on the phone told my partner what to do. He put his hand down there to stop the baby coming out too quickly but I shouted at him to take his hand away as it felt as if he was trying to push the baby back up. When the baby was in my partner's arms, he asked me to move along a bit with him, saying the cable wasn't long enough. The paramedics cut the cord when they arrived and helped us into the ambulance. We were about to make our way to hospital when my husband shouted: "Stop!" He wanted to get out, because he had forgotten to put his teeth in. We made our way to the hospital while my husband followed in our car with his teeth in place." They talked about how I made them feel more relaxed after they had been in shock. I finished giving the woman the care she needed, then fetched them both tea and sandwiches. I stayed with them to allow them both to chat about their experience. The more they laughed about the situation, the more they calmed down. Her partner was over the moon to know he was named as the person who helped deliver their baby.

The midwifery profession in Britain is forever changing. The changes in the next few years will be based on continuity of carer. It is hoped women will have closer relationships with midwives and midwives will have a deeper understanding of the women under their care. In another sense, it is hoped the love-link cord is strengthened to try and enhance the health of women and babies and improve the chances of women having positive experiences and outcomes during pregnancy, labour and birth. It is thought a woman can relax and birth her baby naturally within familiar surroundings or in surroundings they can feel at home in. Some of this theory is based on natural survival instincts of our human element, but I am guessing there is so much more about the hormonal or energy part of us during childbirth we are yet to fully understand.

Places and things retain energy particles which can give off positive or negative energy. I wonder if regular cleansing of stagnant and negative energy in maternity units could help women have more positive outcomes when they opt for a hospital birth. Diffusing aromatherapy or using crystals to absorb, change and give out positive energy are inexpensive natural remedies which could be used. A woman may be able to feel more at home in maternity wards if she takes personal items with her. Photographs or items containing familiar smells and textures such as her dressing gown or her partner's sweatshirt may help her feel more at home.

A profession in the care industry can be very emotional and stressful. My colleagues and I sometimes talk about what we experience and generally wind down with a bit of a laugh when we have our breaks. Tea-time banter can be quite a tonic, especially when the conversation gets below the belt. We often talk about our families during our breaks, because not only do we get personal in a labour room – we can get personal in the tea room, too, especially when funny things happen. One colleague told us her eldest child used his childish logic when he scolded his younger brother: "Remember, mum is a midwife and she can put you back to where you came from."

A student midwife told us she had been caught driving at seventy miles an hour in a thirty-miles-an-hour zone immediately after she had passed her driving test. We asked what possessed her to do that. She replied: "See when you are learning to drive, you can only go thirty!" We were all in stitches, trying to explain to her that thirty is the maximum speed you are ever supposed to drive in builtup areas.

They say Angels can fly because they take themselves lightly. I have felt this happiness in the afterlife so wonder if keeping hilarity in our lives is the way to banish negative emotions like sadness and fear. One midwife is so funny she should write her own book. She brought hilarity regarding the subject of death into the tearoom when she told me about a family funeral she had been to. Her uncle was one of the pall-bearers at the funeral and was using a cord to help lower the coffin. When he leant forward his glasses fell off his face onto the top of the coffin. I asked my colleague if he quickly got them back. She said: "No, he tried to straighten up the coffin with his cord and had to watch his glasses falling to the ground underneath the coffin. His wife could not compose herself and shouted at him: "I've just paid two hundred pounds for those glasses!"

I hope my family manage to 'Keep it Happy' and will demonstrate humour at my funeral. I would not be surprised if they turn around to look at the church door expecting me to come back for my glasses just as I do every time I leave my house. There are so many funny and ironic things which can feed our souls.

After I discussed my experiences of the afterlife, some of my colleagues shared their stories. My colleague Denise previously worked in palliative care and came across a brave man who was terminally ill. He shared his near-death experience with her. He described rising up and reaching the afterlife just as I had done in my past-life regression session. He talked about a vivid place he visited which was full of love and laughter. He told Denise not to be sad for him and not to be afraid of dying, because where we go is a much better place. She told me this man eventually died with a peaceful smile on his face.

There are many people who have not experienced death within their immediate circle or have had any contact with the afterlife so it is understandable that they remain sceptical. This is the reason I chose carefully who I speak to about the afterlife, especially about my most exciting contact with my daughter. My telephone rang when I was deep in thought writing my Heavenly Message poem. I picked up the receiver to hear a loud, screeching, muffled sound shouting: "Mum!" as if the telephone wires had an electrical field running through it. This could very well have been a fault in the line but there were no problems before or after this call. I am aware this is another way Spirit can contact us so took it as a sign of Natalie sending me love and letting me know she was around, regardless of the cause.

HEAVENLY MESSAGE

I have family members, friends and colleagues who have seen and heard their loved ones or smelt odours associated with those they have lost. Some have been sent the kind of little Heavenly Messages I talk about in my poem. Some heavenly messages can be unusual but have a significant meaning for the receiver. People can receive answers to their questions in mysterious ways such as a book falling on the floor, open at an appropriate page or a specific number or words cropping up on everyday items such as car number plates or television programmes.

When I am working, my mind is usually purely on my work. One day, for some reason, I could not get Natalie out of my mind. Somehow, she managed to send me a tiny plastic motif of an owl while I helped a woman birth her baby. The motif did not belong to anyone and the room had been deep-cleaned before we used it. This heavenly message has meaning for me, because Natalie and I were in a shop at a time when we knew she was very ill. I picked up a little pebble which had the picture of an owl and the words "Owl be there for you" painted on it. I bought the pebble and handed it to Natalie. I told her it would be a lovely present for her to give to one of her family members. She turned to me and said: "No, I want to give it to you, Mum!" My heart melted as I struggled to hold back the tears.

My friend and colleague Judith was having a difficult day after the loss of her mum. Her eyes sparkled while she talked about the little white feathers and pennies she receives on a regular basis. She struggles with not having her mum physically in her life but knows her mum is always with her in spirit. Her belief was confirmed before her mum's body was put to rest. She was standing beside her mum's wardrobe full of clothes, deciding what clothes to put on her mum for the funeral. In distress, she called out to her mum to please help her. She could not believe her eyes when a pair of trousers was yanked off a coat hanger in the wardrobe and landed on the floor. She was even more surprised to find the trousers perfectly matched the blouse she had in her hand.

My colleague Christine told me about some of the little signs she had been getting after her father died. She told me her husband refused to believe in the existence of an afterlife or in heavenly messages from Spirit until a little Robin Red-breast visited them. It hopped around, following Christine in her garden for a prolonged time, until she had no doubt it was a heavenly message. I am sure we just have to be open to receive the messages those in the spirit world send us.

I walked over a path full of little white feathers during a woodland walk with my friend Babs. I picked one up and whispered: "A feather a day keeps the blues away." I shared my joy of seeing the feathered pathway with Babs after our walk, but she had failed to see them.

When Cameron and I were out and about, he released his balloon into the sky with a private message for Natalie. He wanted to be sure it would reach his sister so he had me standing with him for quite a while until it disappeared out of sight. He screamed with delight when a feather blew into the open window beside him while we were travelling home in the car. He shouted "Natalie heard me!"

I have found that people from all walks of life talk about the heavenly messages they receive. A nurse was helping me have a hospital treatment when she spotted the draft of my book beside me. She began talking about the afterlife and told me her granddad sends her little feathers regularly. Another time, a young woman was trimming my hair when she told me about the little feathers she finds around her. One family were supporting a woman in labour when they began talking about the feathers they regularly receive from their mother in the spirit world. While giving care to another lovely lady, I noticed a most beautiful lifelike feather with a personal heart-warming message tattooed on her right foot. She told me she had it done in memory of her brother who died at the age of twenty-six. She was happy for me to share her story. During her brother's funeral, a feather suddenly floated down in-front of her and landed at her feet. These stories are not unique. I have come to realise little feathers seem to be the most common gift Spirit sends us as a token of the great love they still hold for us.

Love Always For Everyone

As I think about 'feeling the love' Natalie talked about – the love for everyone and all countries – I realise some people appear removed from their true self and from everyone around them. I understand it can be hard to link with people who we feel have done us wrong and have different beliefs from us. This break in the love-link is causing problems in the world. Many countries are working together to bring back the love-link cords, to make a happier, stronger and safer place to live in.

Some people in well-developed countries can live blinkered lives while they preserve their way of living. A blind eye can be given to poverty, cruelty and the repercussions of war within our world. My eyes are wide open; I have woken from a deep sleep due to the journey of grief and wonder what it will take to wake us all up to link with each other for the sake of there being peace and harmony for all.

Many people are living blind when they use man-made products such as concrete, tarmac and synthetic grass to cover gardens around their homes. They unwittingly deny themselves the natural healing vibrations which real grass, trees and flowers provide. Little creatures cannot survive in these ever-increasing kinds of environment. There may be a knock-on effect for larger creatures which feed off smaller creatures. The domino ripple of a small action can develop into a huge detrimental outcome. If people stepped back from their fast, convenient lives to think about life around them, the decline in our status quo might start to improve.

Global warming is happening now due to our modes of living which are out of sync with Mother Earth. We use chemicals with or without our knowledge of their carcinogenic effects. Substances such as pesticides, cleaning fluid, makeup and perfume all contain chemicals which we inhale into our lungs and absorb through our skin. Some of these substances are excreted out into the circulation of the world. I am not surprised we are suffering so many mutations and illnesses such as Cancer.

Our overuse of gas and electric items, especially phones, iPads and computers is also causing us harm. The more we advance with technology the further it can remove us from our true self. Nevertheless, a certain amount of technology can be seen as a positive advancement in our lives. It has brought many people together and enables everyone to have access to world-wide news. It can help people standing together when positive and negative events occur, raising our vibrations collectively to unknown heights for the greater good. A great number of people have given money to charitable organisations after learning about certain individuals' or establishments' difficulties in the media and over the web. They have come together to help others in trouble or in pain following an illness or a global disaster. Technology can be seen to be helping save parts of the environment as we, perhaps, use less paper and other resources when collating, sending and saving data. Databases can calculate and manipulate data quickly so computers can help us to do what we need to do quickly without great effort. Many people are working from home and are having appointments or interviews over the web so travelling time and costs are reduced or negligible. A meeting or appointment held over the web reduces the likelihood of cross contamination of infections and reduces emissions as no transport is used.

There are so many positive reasons for having technology in our life but excessive use of it can be detrimental to our health. I am not an expert on the harmful vibrations from machines, but I am aware they exist. I was inspired to think about the harm technology is doing to our younger generation when I saw a photo of at least a dozen teenagers huddled together on a couch in the centre of an Art gallery. Every one of them had their heads down, engrossed in their mobile phones instead of looking up and enjoying all the glory in-front of them. Some children reported on a news bulletin of feeling stressed at having to keep a high profile most of the time due to the high prevalence of social media in their lives. Most children use web pages and visual phone calls so do not go through a single day without using technology of some sort.

When children are face-to-face with whom they are talking to, they can see the hurt they cause when they say spiteful things. When they talk over the web the physical human interaction is lost, so upsetting messages can be sent by the touch of a button without the consequences being apparent. A support group reported that there has been an upsurge of phone calls from children, some of whom are self-harming, asking for help. It is believed that some children feel isolated due to not having sufficient interaction with their parents and family. It is thought these family members are regularly occupied and distracted on their phones and other electronic devices. Subsequently, this preoccupation denies children the kind of social interaction which can enhance their sense of self, inner strength and ability to cope with life.

I have been guilty of allowing my older children to be babysat by television programmes and more recently allowed Cameron to be occupied by his iPad. It can take much negotiation and bribing to detach him from it. As I watch my son being engrossed in his iPad instead of being outside, fishing for tadpoles or playing hide and seek, I wonder if this universal problem will only get worse without intervention. People are well-connected to each other in a technological way, but in a personal and vibration sense, they may be becoming detached from their inner self and estranged from those who are physically around them.

I am sure my Unit is no different from other work establishments when there can be great silences at break times while mobile phones are being used. My intuition and healing ability is stronger when I am with other sensitive people and away from technology. Our internal awareness and spiritual energy are naturally boosted when we connect with other people in a positive manner. In contrast, we close down our hearts and energy systems to protect ourselves from harmful vibrations, especially when we are being ignored or hurt by something or someone.

We have learned so much about our human physical bodies in such a few years. It is mind-boggling to think how much more we may be able to learn in the future. Much of what is being shared recently regarding the vibration element of our being has been known since ancient times and can be read about in many books. However, the acceptance of it within the wider population has taken a great deal longer due to the constraints of external influences such as the lack of physical evidence of its existence. The full effect of technology on our energy system and general well-being is yet to be known. As a published researcher, I am still trying to fathom how physical evidence for a non-physical phenomenon can be proven without doubt.

There is the belief that the endocrine pineal gland in the centre of our brain is our third eye and is linked to our spiritual being and connection with all living people and things. It is thought to be the source of our spiritual abilities and governs our level of health. The higher the vibration of this gland, the better our health is and the easier we can connect with our spiritual energy and of that of others on Earth and beyond our physical world. Sunlight and meditation enhances the vibration of our pineal gland and darkness enables it to rest. Jennifer Luke did research which showed how the chemical sodium fluoride has a detrimental effect on the pineal gland. She explored the theory that fluoride calcifies the gland to such an extent our ability to use our inner power is diminished. She suggests this calcification can cause harm to our bodies. The benefits of fluoride making our teeth stronger, justifies the practice of fluoride being added to our drinking and bath water and into our food and beverages. I guess it is up to the individual to research these issues more to come to their own conclusions.

It has been suggested that there is valid research to prove our spiritual energy exists but I have not found any evidence. However, there is a group of mediums who are currently taking part in research in America, and the results of their research may help us to step closer to the proof we are all looking for. A closer look at Laura Lynn Jackson's book called "The Light Between Us" will enlighten people more about this research. I am sure there are many more research projects which will come to light in the near future.

I chose a research project about nausea and vomiting in pregnancy for my dissertation when studying for my Honours Degree in midwifery. This condition has been highlighted in the media due to the Duchess of Cambridge having the condition whilst she was pregnant. It was difficult to find hard evidence for the facts I tried to relay on the issues surrounding it all. I discussed aids which could help such as pressing on specific points in the meridian system to block the energy flow at specific points in the body. I now ponder on the process of the foetal energy system linking with the maternal energy system and wonder if the mother's condition is exacerbated by both energy fields being out of sync as they co-exist and begin to merge.

Each person contains a varied and constant interchangeable balance of the opposing Yin and Yang energy in our bodies. This Chi energy is linked to every part of our body components and its' functions. It connects with our environment and every living thing around us. Perhaps the balance of a pregnant woman's energy could be changed to be more in-line with their baby's energy. Aligning maternal and fetal Chi energy fields might reduce the feeling of being out of balance and improve the symptoms of nausea and vomiting. It could be researched whither certain factors could bring about change. It is already known that our Yang energy is increased when we are in warmer climates, doing physical activities and eating hot food. Yin energy can be increased by being in a cooler environment, reducing physical energy and sleeping more. The balance of Yin energy within us can be further increased by enjoying mental pursuits such as reading and meditating, drinking more fluids and eating cold food.

Aligning maternal and fetal energy systems could be thought to be achievable when we explore psychic activities which change the molecular structure of our energy systems. Some mediums talk about the process of trans-shadowing and transfiguration. Trans-shadowing is a process where Spirit uses a medium's energy field to superimpose a vision of the Spirit's human body as they were known when living. Transfiguration is where Spirit enters the medium's human body to alter its shape to mimic Spirit's appearance. In the latter case, Spirit uses the medium's body chemicals to adjust their own vibrations so they can merge with the medium's body. This process can cause the medium to feel nauseated, out of balance, drained, light-headed and dehydrated. We know these are the symptoms of nausea and vomiting in pregnancy and it is treated by bed-rest, administering anti-sickness drugs and intravenous fluids. It would be an interesting research project, but it may probably be near impossible to prove that there could be a link with the condition and the body's energy systems due to our limited knowledge and understanding of it all. One thing may have absolutely nothing to do with the other, but it would be interesting to see what effects meditation, manipulation of our chemicals and energy vibrations would have on women suffering with this condition.

Many of us resort to taking prescribed medications for our ailments rather than delve into our natural healing methods. I laughed with my colleagues as I discussed how people in some countries start their working day with manipulating their energy systems, but where we live, some of us start our day by taking oral pain killers. Many professional establishments could benefit from offering energy vibration pursuits and therapies such as shiatsu, taichi or aromatherapy, but the lack of valid research usually deters anything of this nature from being offered due to fear of litigation. In other words, research facilitates regulations, guidelines and polices to keep people safe and help reduce the likelihood of a company or establishment being sued. The fear of losing money through these means would be enough to put anyone in business off using energy vibration healing methods.

I have worked with healing or light energy for over twenty-five years. A light or energy worker was not an option given to me when I was sat down at school and asked what occupation I would like to study for. I do think this kind of therapy, along with other alternative therapies, could be included more when career options are discussed. Incorporating these therapies in schools could help young ones cope in an ever-increasing stressful world full of new dangers to health which people my age never experienced. Introducing healing therapy into schools could be viewed as pioneering as the therapy Pierre Dulaine brought into the education system. He designed the Dulaine method of teaching dance in classrooms in order to increase children's social and emotional development and is still widely used today.

Every single person and living thing has the ability to heal. I believe there is more to a child cuddling a teddy and people embracing each other than we understand. The chemicals of our body mix and merge just like the chemical components of loose and free substances like steam or smoke. I am guessing that everything comes down to interchangeable molecules which are part of our seven body layers, including the physical body. If our physical bodies were solid and did not continually change, we would never grow up, get old, get ill, heal or die. Living plants and flowers contain similar healing chemical vibrations which mix and react with ours. This is why we use them to make aromatherapy or Bach-flower healing products.

I know nothing of the galaxy and what goes on out there, but I am sure there will be molecules involved with the study of it all. When studying for my Crystal Therapy Degree I read that it was a therapy which was a science yet to be discovered. This statement could be given to all healing therapies. It is interesting how crystals grow and have a healing effect on us, but they are not classed as living. There is so much around us which we are yet to understand.

My colleague's husband is a gifted healer like me but only gives my colleague treatments at home because of his beliefs. I met a gifted psychic medium who was in turmoil about her ability to receive messages from spirit. She refused to pass on these important messages to anyone due to her beliefs. It is possible that the discouragement of psychic and healing activities within some circles may be caused by the emotion Fear. Much fear can be born from a lack of knowledge or understanding. This fear may date back to the times of the great witch hunt when people with psychic powers were thought to be practicing witch-craft and cavorting with the devil. Both psychic and non-psychic people vary in their opinion whether psychic activity is a religious phenomenon or not. I am aware everyone has to come to their own conclusions about our energy systems and the afterlife according to their own beliefs, but it is hard for me to comprehend why some people feel it is wrong to use their own ability to heal in a more natural, less damaging and least expensive way. Changing the way we view ourselves and our inner abilities could be the key which could unlock the closed door for us to reach unknown great potential.

There is a new generation of children who are here to try and change our views and ways of living. They are trying to wake us up by raising our awareness and our vibrations. They come with memories of existing before they arrived here in their present life. They bring astonishing proof about the afterlife and reincarnation. Some of them were televised on a programme called 'The Ghost inside my Child.' Having knowledge of having been a different person in a previous life can cause upset and turmoil for them and their families. Some children remember living in a body with the opposite gender and have contacted health professionals to help them accept their present gender or discuss changing it.

Cameron never fails to surprise me with some of the things he says. The two of us were sitting on a train on our way to visit my parents, when he was in deep conversation with a lovely lady sitting across from us. He told her his sister is in Heaven, followed by: "When I was in Heaven, I was deciding to be born, not to be born, to be born, and not to be born" in a matter-of-fact manner. This took me by surprise as I had indeed had a few miscarriages before being pregnant with him. Initially, we were told he had no heart-beat, and near the end of my confinement, I had an event which could have resulted in him not surviving. When I was reading him a bedtime story about a bear making a rocket to go to the moon and stars he began telling me: "When I was in Heaven, I was looking down at all the mummies and daddies and was choosing what one to have." I looked at him, trying to hide my surprise: "What made you choose me?" He replied with a big cuddle: "I just liked you. I knew you would be kind and would look after me. Then I went into your tummy and went to sleep. I felt nothing, and then I was here." When my father-in-law passed away, Cameron looked at me less than an hour after his death and informed me: "I have just talked to Grandad and told him to look after Natalie."

Cameron is like many children who are aware of spirit. The satnav in my car was not working so a taxi driver kindly took Cameron, my mum and I to a hospital for Cameron to have an emergency appointment while we were on holiday at Sandylands Holiday Park in Ayrshire. During the journey, the taxi driver took great pleasure in telling us he found his young son in bed, sitting bold upright, wide awake chatting to the taxi driver's dad who had recently died.

There are many questions surrounding life after death which remain unanswered. Some mediums believe children grow up in heaven, some talk about Sprits choosing to appear around the optimum age of thirty years. Other psychic people believe when Spirit are in contact with loved ones on Earth, they can show themselves at whatever age we expect them to be. My human brain remains confused with some of the issues as I have read about many conflicting opinions and experiences. While reading 'A Baby's Viewpoint of Life and Death' by Anita Lavato and Dr James Wilkins, I learned about the viewpoint of life after death from a little girl who had died. She shared insight and wisdom regarding life and the afterlife which appeared to be far greater knowledge than a small child would understand. All I know is that when I saw my daughter in the afterlife, she had all the characteristics of my daughter but was also a spirit of many characters and of all ages.

Entities from the afterlife are reaching out to us while people on Earth are coming together in many different ways to try and prove that we go on living after we leave our bodies. I kept my knowledge, beliefs and ability regarding the afterlife and alternative therapies at home away from my working life for fear of being viewed as being different or unprofessional, just as many people like me have done. I generally do not cross the boundary of purposely and openly using my ability to help people at my work through healing or with any other alternative therapy unless it is requested. It is my responsibility as a midwife to be non-judgmental and keep my opinions and beliefs out of a delivery room, but if a woman under my care initiates a conversation surrounding spiritual or psychic matters I will discuss it.

One woman required a caesarean section to deliver her baby after quite a long labour. I could see she was exhausted and anxious while we waited for theatre to be made ready for her. She told me she was used to having alternative therapy sessions so I offered her a healing session to help her rest peacefully while we waited. The woman and her mother thanked me a few days later and were happy for me to share that they felt the healing made the woman calm enough to face going into theatre. Some women have received Healing or Reiki therapy while waiting to go to theatre to have their placenta delivered after normal procedures failed to expel it. Unfortunately, there has been no research done to show the effectiveness of the therapy aiding the delivery of retained placentas.

Some of my work colleagues were sceptical about the benefits of healing until they heard of others I had helped. They began asking me to take ten minutes or so out of my busy work schedule to give them a healing so they could continue with their day. Not everyone can be healed, but I will try if I am asked. I usually feel energy between my hands and the recipient so in the rare cases when I feel nothing, I know healing is not to take place at that particular time. Sometimes, we have an illness or condition to make us follow a certain road or take a particular U-turn in our route of life. Illnesses or imperfections may occur to slow us down, make us rest for a while or open our eyes to something. Sometimes, it is a nudge or a sign for us to help other people.

Many of us cause our illnesses by having poor diets and making poor health choices. The increase of carbohydrates and sugar in our diets is causing a rise in the amount of people who have health problems such as diabetes, heart defects and infertility. The health of our nation is now a major concern as a result. More worryingly, the continuation of the human race could be at risk if we do not change what we eat.

In midwifery, part of the programme 'Best Start' is working towards improving the health of new generations even before they are born by looking at maternal preconception care. Nurseries and Schools are working with children to improve their diet and way of life. We as adults have the responsibility to provide optimum opportunities to help our children flourish and reach their potential. Opportunity is like a clear night sky which is required to allow children to shine like the stars they are.

Cameron's school is working hard to get back to basics where it comes to children's physical, mental and spiritual health. They encourage children to get to school by walking, cycling or riding their scooter. They have after-school sports activities such as gymnastics, badminton and athletics to keep the youngsters fit. The school has an outside classroom to help children learn in a non-constricting natural environment. Cameron has a motivated teacher who encourages learning by using sensory means. He takes the children out of school into the community to give lessons as he knows children learn in this way without realising they are learning. The best part of the school's theology is that they discourage parents and guardians from collecting their children while using their mobile phones and encourage them to put their computers off at home and enjoy time with their children. Spending quality time with children by enjoying a game of tennis, playing a board game or taking a trip to a local park all costs very little or nothing at all.

Cameron loves going on family bike rides, and his iPad gets chucked instantly when he sees me getting our bikes out. I often ponder over the reason for children not playing outside as much as they did in my day. There have always been people surrounding children who should not be, but technology and the Wide World News have created a bigger awareness of cases of harm and abuse. This makes parents like me keep our children within sight, disallowing them to have the freedom to roam and explore the way we once did. Construction developments which flattened our landscapes have also limited the adventures our children can have.

I took Cameron to a play-park which had a stream full of life when I was young. I enjoyed many days looking at the plant life and watching the tiny fish and frogs. The park had been reduced to a fraction of its size and the stream turned into a muddy ditch full of discarded rubbish. The stream had been divided for a road to lead up to the large expensive houses which were built on the park-land. Many wooded areas I played in have been replaced with housing estates. When cuts are being made to save money within a town, recreational facilities are usually the first to go. I am sure the repercussions of closing Community Centres and leisure facilities, reducing or demolishing play and recreational areas where wild life once lived has been grossly underestimated.

I am not an expert in the world of nature, but I was interested to learn about the astounding repercussions which occurred when a pack of wolves were re-settled onto an area of wilderness. The equilibrium of the land and wildlife was naturally restored. Many of us could learn from this project as it would be ignorant of us as human beings to believe that we can be sole survivors on Earth. The physical impact of the loss of living things from our world is being considered world-wide, but the break in the energy link with them is not. Science in this sense has not caught up with the spiritual energy link with nature and animals which Aboriginal descendants have embraced since the beginning of time.

There are wildlife programmes in some countries where creatures are given a helping hand to survive and increase their numbers. In Trinidad, children are taught how to protect the Leatherback turtle, and adults have been involved in helping the turtles overcome some of the dangers which threaten their survival. Species are killed for unnecessary and unlawful reasons and the foods they eat are being diminished needlessly. The real danger to most plant life and creatures lies in the problems which humans create.

Seas, rivers and ponds have been polluted by the chemicals and rubbish we have discarded into them over the years and as a result, plant and animal life has reduced or fails to exist. It was highlighted on television that research has been done by two hundred and fifty scientists over eight years to show there has been a steep rise in temperatures and carbon dioxide which has caused parts of the ocean to be more acidic. Young sea life appears to be more sensitive to carbon dioxide so cannot survive the toxic levels. As a result, large areas of the coral reef have been turned into white bleached crumbling deserts. The damage could be reversed by reducing the amount of carbon dioxide levels we emit into the atmosphere.

Some people in houses and establishments are causing pollution needlessly. I watched a man throw rubbish out of his garden gate onto a well-used country walkway where I live. This man must have believed the rubbish was out of his life, but it wasn't going anywhere. It was still outside his door and all the negative energy, thoughts or vibrations people had about the rubbish being there as they walked past it would rebound back to him. The wildlife which inhabits the countryside beside his home may also have been harmed by his pollution.

The huge rise in emissions from the increased numbers of vehicles on our roads has added to the pollution we live with, while the safety of our children around our roads is of equal concern. I wonder if we would benefit from having some no-through roads, dead-end roads if there are alternative routes. These could be play spots around our homes, areas where our children could play more safely in our streets.

There are organisations which strive to encourage individuals and staff in schools to take their children outdoors to explore and play. Organisations like Wild Time Learning and the National Trust RSPB aim to entice children to spend time in natural surroundings, away from technology. It is thought children might enjoy the sensory experience of the great outdoors and may take more of an interest in preserving nature and our wild life if they are exposed to it during childhood.

Staff at Cameron's school encouraged me to take him out and about to play as part of his homework. He enjoyed going to a wooded area with a list of things to find. He was to invent an animal which has two parts of a different species which could live in the woods. He was to give his animal a name, make a drawing or painting of it and build it a home to live in. I loved his idea of a Batbird called Chirpy and was even more impressed with his painting of his animal. He was in his element, cheerfully singing while we painted his Batbird tree-house together.

Artistic pursuits are known to relax and stretch the mind to allow our spirit to connect with other living people and things, to feel happy and free. I was inspired by the wonderful time I spent with Cameron to write a poem. The poem was used to create a delightful children's book called 'My Little Friend Batbird.' I created six other dual animal creatures with the illustrator Sofania, to help encourage children to leave their iPads at home and go out into the world with their family and explore.

Natalie's Song

My journey of grief may have no end. I may only learn to live with it. There are no footprints to follow; we all have to make our own individual way back to life. I emerged from the deeper depths and darker days of my journey but no matter how much I tried to move on with my life, I wanted my daughter to be remembered somehow. I needed to show how the love-link with our lost loved ones never dies. When I showed my Heavenly Message poem to Natalie's friends, they told me the words sounded like a song.

This gave me an idea. I asked my friend Lorna, if her partner would be interested in composing a song for me out of the poem. Her partner, Lino G Rocha, is a wonderful soulful lead singer with Son al Son and Salsa Celtica. Lino came to my house to discuss it and began making the song. He changed some of the words so the song could have meaning for other people who have lost a loved one. He went to Croatia to work on theatrical projects with his musical partner Andrej Kljakovic, one of which is a multi-media musical called Tesla Rock Opera yet to be released. While Lino was there, he recorded our song with Oleg Colnago, Andrej Kljakovic, Ivan Penza, Penezic and Martin Mandic who are all well-known in their own country. The company, A1D London Ltd, produced the discs professionally for us so we could sell hard copies of the song and Lino made it available for sale on websites such as Amazon. The song was released for the first anniversary of Natalie's death. I pledged my share of the profit of the song to go to The Eilidh Brown Memorial Fund which was set up in memory of Natalie's friend who also died of Cancer. The medium Diane White told me Natalie wanted me to know she was extremely happy she would be remembered for a long time with the song and my book.

Heavenly Message: **Natalie's Song**

Here I am, yet another long night
filled with memories good and bad.
I close my eyes to see your face
and remember all the times we had.
And looking down it brought a smile,
I held you close and sensed the wonder
of your stunning grace.

I saw you blossom through the years
with great beauty, awe and might.
You stole the hearts of many souls;
you stood like shining pearls of light.
I know the tears will always be by my side,
when I think of all the years there could have been,
you could have had,
and feel your loving by my side.

There will be Rainbows, white feathers,
butterflies and flying birds at play in an open sky.
There will be songs on the radio
in glorious stereo
and bright lights flickering away.

All I know that makes it real
is the love that we can share,
to feel your arms around me,
to feel your smile surround me
and knowing you will always be there.

There will be Rainbows, white feathers,
butterflies and flying birds at play in an open sky.
There will be songs on the radio
in glorious stereo
and bright lights flickering away.

Spiritual Elements

Lino made a video to accompany the song and when we watched the footage of him on YouTube singing in the recording studio we could see little bright circles dashing around. I initially thought they might have been caused by dazzling lights in the studio but they were so random, darting in many different directions at a high speed. Lino informed me that there was only one static light in the studio, much the same as a household ceiling light. There were no spinning globes or mirrors which could have reflected the lights into the singing booth. Spirit told me they would be with us when we produced the song, so I guess these little bright circles were, in-fact, pure energy orbs. I am aware it takes great effort and energy for spirits to show themselves as we knew them when they were alive, so many of them appear in the simple form of an orb – a ball of light.

My friend and colleague Sharon told me she was staying with her sister the day after her father's funeral. She was sitting in the living-room when she witnessed a round bright light drawing towards her. It lingered for a while before it dashed upstairs towards her sister's bedroom where her sister lay sleeping. She felt an overwhelming familiar love emanating from this light so believed it was her father coming close to her to give her reassurance and to say 'goodbye'. My colleague Julie showed me a picture she has of spirit orbs her cat was playing with. When a hospital porter overheard our conversation, he told us orbs surrounded him every day. While enjoying the MHT comedy Drag Dinner Show in Tenerife, Andy and I became friendly with a couple who talked about their contact with Spirit and showed us an impressive photo they took of many bright spirit orbs of varying sizes in their livingroom.

Spirit orbs often come close to us during our daily living. The first time I saw one was when I visited a medium in Inverness. It was bright white and encased in a brighter circular light, approximately the size of a dinner plate. There appeared to be a smaller orb within it. Their purpose is to send us love, healing, guidance and protection. I often see these orbs when mediums are relaying messages or giving healing from Spirit. I was in awe the first time I saw a spirit orb within and behind a medium's head at the Spiritualist Church, while she relayed spiritual advice to the congregation. I regularly see mediums' auras expanding and retracting when they link and interact with Spirit's energy. I watched a medium work in-front of a large audience at the Golden Lion Hotel in Stirling recently. I could see when her link with Spirit's energy was strong and when it was weak. The spirit light linked with her aura and they both appeared to be bright and sold when spirit messages were being given to the audience then dim and transparent, like flowing smoke as the link tapered off.

It makes sense to me that there may have been spirits on the other side who were around us when the song was made, just as my daughter has been around me, sending me thoughts to be put into words in my book. Other people have had the experience of famous people who have passed into the afterlife helping them write their books or songs. Gary Gentry is a co-writer of the song called The Ride. He claims that the spirit of Hank Williams helped him write the song. The actor Mel Gibson is said to have been given help from an unearthly source with his block- buster film called 'The Passion of The Christ.'

As I was writing about the 'Tesla Rock Opera' Lino is involved in, I heard a voice tell me: "It will take extraordinary measures to change extraordinary circumstances, the people should know." I wondered what Spirit was talking about so I researched what Tesla's life and work was about. Tesla made discoveries about time and space which could be influenced by manipulating magnetic fields, and he called them time-zone experiments. He claimed to have received radio signals from outside the planet and was involved in mind-blowing phenomena such as the 'Philadelphia Experiment.' Much of his work had been confiscated and hidden. Some authorities did not want the general public to know about his work so much of his research findings and inventions were disregarded. The knowledge he tried to give the world could be the extraordinary measures we all need to start changing our ways for the better, for the greater good of all.

We are already using fewer plastic products and aerosol-based goods. Some of us recycle what we discard and there are policies working towards reducing emissions. Some people have embarked on campaigns to raise awareness of our wrong-doings towards our planet. I wonder whether there are those who are becoming more displaced from themselves and from the natural world around them by being fixated with having products in their lives they could easily do without. There is so much more we can do for ourselves to improve the world we all live in. It has to begin with finding the love within ourselves and those around us. Perhaps, we could all be a part of trying to help improve our communities with good community spirit, a kind of bonding in the community which generates a sense of belonging.

My village tries to involve its inhabitants in the decisions made for change and improvement, and some people are actively involved in a flood watch, making sure the river and countryside by us is free from debris and pollution. A few years ago, I watched residents of my village plant many flowers together. The sight of those wonderful plants and colourful blooms as I reached home after my four-hour arduous commutes from work lifted my spirits and probably sent positive thought vibrations back to all those who had taken the time to create the lovely display.

Love and life in general are like the flowers which grew in that village. When a flower grows from a tree it evolves from a bud and enjoys its full bloom when in its prime. It wilts and falls to the ground and returns back to its source after its reason for being is complete. When you look at a flower growing from the ground do you only see one pretty petal or see all the petals in full bloom? Do you see the stem and roots it grows from and the earth, rain and sun which help it thrive? Do you see the other plants, the people, the animals and the buildings surrounding it? Are you aware of the village and country it lives in and the cosmic sky towering over it? Are you able to look deeper and feel its energy vibrations reaching out and touching you? We are like the single petal of a flower; we cannot come to be or continue to exist alone. Like a drop in an ocean, without the other drops we would be next to nothing. Collectively, we make a whole, we live together and how we live our lives affects everyone.

Just as all living things, the flower's subtle energy can flourish or diminish in response to its surroundings. This substance is not solid matter so it can reach out beyond the scope of our horizons like smoke in a breeze. It is the part of us which merges and interacts with every living person and living thing. It can enable us to have telepathic thoughts with other people and it could be the reason why we are able to communicate with our spirit guide and our loved ones in the spirit world. This linking of our spiritual energy reminds me of a string of cut-out paper dolls, all in a row, each with a separate identity but none separate from the others.

The amount of spiritual or subtle energy we all have as a whole is huge. One physical body cannot house that magnitude level of energy; our body would probably spontaneously combust if it tried to. We generally contain around twenty percent of our collective energy within our human vessel. We each have varying levels of spiritual energy within us as we all have had different experiences and are at different levels of development in our soul's journey. The amount of energy we choose to bring with us can depend on our soul's life purpose.

My hypnotherapy session with Paul allowed me to feel this energy within me as it linked with Natalie, my dad and spirit guide. I have felt it when giving healing to people, animals and plants here on Earth, but I had never before dipped into the afterlife to feel it on the other side, in the magnitude that it is. Many of us believe this is the energy or spiritual part of us which is no longer present in our physical bodies when we die. Our bodies are two and a quarter pounds lighter after death so this is thought to be the weight of our being which returns to source. It is debatable, but some people are of the opinion that when we return to source we don't actually travel anywhere but merely have the sensation of going through a tunnel or over a bridge as we go through the sensations of transition from our physical body to our spiritual existence.

I was given the gift of feeling the soul energy of my daughter leave her body just before her human body tried to take a last breath. In contrast, I witness babies in my working life taking their first breath as they come into this life. This makes me believe there is more to the phenomena of birth, death and the afterlife than most of us may ever understand. Scores of us have seen or felt this energy leave the body of our loved ones so know it exists. The only way we usually believe and understand all the issues surrounding our energy or spiritual being and the afterlife is to experience it for ourselves. No amount of reading or telling of tales may make us believe it otherwise.

There are many people who believed the point of death is the end of our existence and have had their beliefs upturned when they experience the essence of themselves live on outside their shell or body in near-death experiences and through ground- breaking hypnotherapy sessions. Some of those people have felt so strongly about their experiences that they have written about them so others can see what they have seen.

I did not discuss my experience of working with energy and my contact with Spirit and the afterlife with anyone before losing my daughter. I was like many who fear being ridiculed by people who are completely closed to the idea of it all. My understanding of healing energy has been a gradual process through my life so I can relate to people who have no understanding of it. I believe it really is a science yet to be discovered rather than being a form of magic, witchcraft, faith or a kind of religion. In the past, it was thought copper could be turned to gold by dowsing it in a magic substance. In time, science proved it was only a chemical reaction changing the colour of the coin. However, just because we have very little knowledge of something does not make it less so, and because something is a certain way does not necessarily mean it should be. I do not understand everything about the car I drive, but it does not stop me from using it to get to where I want to be, just as I use healing energy without full knowledge of it. Many minds need to open for our collective energy to flow, to connect with each other and heal. Perhaps, people like me and miracle workers like the great Healers Betty Shine, Steward Keeys and Charlie Goldsmith are sharing what we have experienced to help open people's closed minds.

I have had the light poured into my life, knowing my daughter lives on in another realm. I have always known we live on after death, but I needed to understand and rationalise it more after losing her. Natalie told me she could see everyone so this made me wonder how Spirit could be in many places at once. She told me time is not linear as we perceive it on Earth and spirits are like hares dashing around us while we, in our 'tortoise physical avatar bodies' go about our business at a painfully slow pace. The high vibration she and other departed loved ones have make it difficult for some people to see, sense and hear them, similar to a highpitched sound we can't hear but a dog can. To try and teach us all the ins and outs of Spirit and the afterlife is like trying to teach a new-born baby to fly a rocket to the moon. To be able to reach Spirit we have to raise our vibrations by slowing down our mind and bodily functions while spirits lower their energy to meet us in the middle.

Altering and Using Energy Vibrations

We can use physical and non-physical modes of manipulating and altering our energy and the energy around us. Some people use physical tools such as crystals. Different crystals are used for various purposes according to their colour and properties. Each crystal colour is linked to the chakras colours of the body. When crystals are cleansed, neutralised and charged properly they can help us clear and heighten our vibrations so we can communicate and work with spirit more effectively. Crystals should be cleansed and charged before and after every use when they are used in healing therapies of the body and mind. If they are worn on a regular basis, they should be touching the skin of the body and be cleansed and charged no less than weekly. We should also be cleansing them weekly if they are used on a regular basis in our homes or in other environments around us. It must be noted that crystals can interfere with technology so should be kept away from products such as watches, ipads, computers and mobile phones.

Most crystals can be cleansed by holding them under running clean cold water but aventurine and citrine can be damaged if they are exposed to water. Burying crystals in sea salt within a small container or wrapping the them in a cloth and burying them in the earth for a minimum of twenty-four hours can give the same effect. Some people like to clean crystals by smudging them with incense smoke, Herbalists use sage herbs and Aromatherapist wipe them with oils such as frankincence.

After cleansing, crystals can be charged in many ways. They can be placed in a singing bowl while the ringing sound of the bowl is created or put on an amethyst crystal bed overnight. Some people sit them under moonlight overnight on a window ledge. They can be programmed and charged by cupping them in our hands until we feel our own energy linking with them.

Clear quartz is a universal crystal which can substitute most crystals. They can be used to heal most ailments, clear stagnant energy and change our energy to create the best environment to meditate, communicate with spirit and work with spiritual energy. I use crystal layouts with clear quarts around my client's bodies when giving crystal healing. I place dark crystals such as obsidian at the feet of my clients to help ground them and purple crystals such as amethyst near their crown to help open their third eye and encourage their ability to self heal. I have placed rose quartz in areas of my home where I hoped to improve energy vibrations. Some people like to burn or smudge incense to clear energy or diffuse aromatherapy before they meditate or work with energy without using crystals. It is advisable to open a window when clearing stagnant energy as this enables negative vibrations to be brushed out of the window.

I have a ritual I use to clear negative energy when moving into a new home or when I feel my home needs a clear-out. I open all the windows while I de-clutter and clean the house thoroughly. I then clap my hands as I walk around each room anti-clockwise to break up and brush out stagnant and negative energy. I take care not to miss clearing out corners, nooks and crannies. I place a lit candle with fresh flower petals into a bowl and put the bowl in the middle of the space I am clearing. I walk clockwise around each room, ringing my bell or sounding my singing bowl to imprint positive energy. Replacing positive energy can also be done by singing or playing high vibration music, because the results are more dependent on the intent than the method used. This ritual can protect our energy when people visit our homes as they can suck our energy away or leave negative energy behind. It is also a helpful ritual for people who feel depressed and want to lift their spirits.

Our surroundings and the people around us can have a huge impact on how we feel on a daily basis. I like to have a small amount of sea salt in a container while giving healing treatments to absorb the client's negative energy. I discard the salt when the treatment is complete by taking it out of the house and burying it into the earth. The earth's dirt can absorb and raise the vibrations of the salt again. Many people burn incense or scented candles to rid their homes of negative energy and raise its vibrations.

I often use aromatherapy oil to heighten my energy vibrations and the vibrations around me. I am aware that some clients may have allergies or contra-indications to some aromatherapy essential oils so I prefer to wait until they are present before I use them in treatments. I find that combining aromatherapy, crystals and healing energy while giving massage or reflexology treatments enhances the effects of the therapy tenfold. Occasionally, I diffuse essential oils when I am sending absent healing or am meditating to link with Spirit.

The messages I receive from Spirit come in many guises. The mode in which I receive a message from Spirit very much depends on the reason and urgency of them. The most direct communication I have been given is when I have heard clear loud messages as if someone was next to me speaking the words. The most common communication I have had with Spirit is in the form of thought projection. This is where words, pictures and symbols are passed to me like thoughts in my head. The visions of events are like watching sections of a movie show. Energy can be projected to give me a sense of something or someone, these are situations when I know information about something or someone but don't understand why or how I know. I have also seen and felt the vibrations of spirit but I am sure this is to help me understand more about how Spirit communicates and healing energy works.

We are all born with the ability to communicate with Spirit, but many people close themselves down due to the illusion of our physical human life while growing up. Spirit can hear our thoughts regardless of where we are or what state of mind we are in. We generally need to be in a relaxed state of mind for us to hear them unless it is an urgent message being relayed to us. Spending time in wooded areas and at a beach, can help us calm and clear our minds. However, concentrating too hard on reaching our guides can have the opposite effect as our minds would not be in a relaxed state.

Many people use meditation to change and raise their internal energy vibrations. Meditation is a nonphysical method of enabling us to escape our busy world, to recharge our energies and be at one with ourselves. It provides the optimum conditions for us to work out our own problems, regardless of whether we link with our spirit guides or not. We can experience better results and focus better when we meditate regularly. Some people choose to shut themselves away in a room in quietness while meditating for a designated amount of time. Some people like to listen to recordings of directed meditations or chant words or sounds.

When I am meditating, I like to use visualisation techniques. I use one main one with adaptations according to my reason for taking time out. It involves following a path in my mind while in a relaxed state. These techniques are used to self-heal or to find solutions to problems by reaching our inner self with or without trying to reach a higher source. Visualisations may not work for everyone, but it is worth trying different scenarios or pathways.

We can also use other methods to obtain guidance. I have used a crystal pendulum for spiritual guidance just as our ancestors held a needle on a thread when they asked if the baby in their uterus was a girl or a boy. A circle movement indicated a girl and side-to-side movement a boy. I hold the pendulum by its chain at fulllength and take a few deep breaths to still my hand holding the pendulum and raise my awareness. I ask my inner self and spirit what mode of spinning means 'yes' and what means 'no'. I have found circular spinning usually means 'yes', side-to-side means 'no', erratic movements mean the question cannot be answered at present. No movement usually means the question cannot or will not be answered for reasons beyond our understanding.

I have used this method when I was unsure of what oils or crystals to use for a client's condition when research into the condition was not helpful. I also slowly moved a pendulum over a map of Scotland to find out which area was best for me to buy a house. We can write charts with possible answers to our questions and guide a pendulum over the chart to have our higher self or Spirit guide give us the probable answer or outcome. This method can be used to ask many kinds of questions, but – ultimately – everything is about moderation so it would not be healthy or productive to over-use it. It would be similar to phoning your friend a hundred times a day until your friend advises you to seek your answers elsewhere.

Sometimes, we search for answers from spirit, not realising the answers may already be within our hearts. Artistic pursuits like dancing, singing, playing music, painting and writing can help us relax our minds to reach our inner soul for guidance. I enjoy doing all these activities but find writing to be the best mode of relaxation for me at this time.

It can be therapeutic for us to write our problems on a piece of paper and then burn the paper. Many people write letters to reach their higher self or the heart and soul of someone still living. More commonly, letters are written to reach loved ones who are in spirit before the letters are burnt. We can be assured that Spirit will receive our messages, no matter how we write our letters and whether we burn them or send them up into the sky or not.

Laura Turnbull Fyfe who wrote 'Wellspring *tap into your boundless creativity'* taught me how to tap into my inner self by writing for exactly six minutes. Writing constantly for six minutes without stopping, even if it is to write nonsense, can stretch our minds and help our creativity to flow. This is a method some writers use in conjunction with writers' cubes or cards to find prompts or leads for what they would like to write about. Some mediums use this method to find out if automatic writing is a skill they are suited to, but they usually write for hours rather than minutes. When I wrote for six minutes, it helped me express feelings and desires from deep within. This exercise may be able to help others bring out emotions which may have been 'swept under the carpet' rather than 'brushed out the door'.

Some people use this method to help them realise their preferred direction and goal in life. After all, it may be difficult for Spirit to help us achieve our goals if we don't know what they are ourselves. Once our goals are realised, some mediums advise that we should write them down in a positive manner and in the present tense as if we already have what we wish for. We should keep our wish-list beside us for a few months or more to help us achieve them or adjust the list if and when we have attained what we wish for or have new goals. It must be said that some wishes may never be achieved, because there are times they may not be what we really need or they may be considered counter-productive for our soul's purpose in life. Some mediums state that there are too many third-dimensional cosmic requests or ordering being made. This is where people strive to reach selfish and self-indulgent goals rather than try to enhance their human qualities or improve life for everyone.

Out of the many messages Natalie and other spirits gave me, one hit a cord with me the most. Natalie said: "If everyone did a little, it would amount to a lot." If we all had a better understanding of our own vibrations and the science of what we give out coming back to us like a ripple-effect, perhaps we would think twice about our affirmations, our life choices and how we treat everyone and everything around us.

I related this message to an experience I had while on holiday in Mallorca. My family and I were staying nextdoor to an extremely loud, argumentative family who had been fuelled by the all-inclusive drinks from the two hotel bars. The couple shouted at each other and at their very young toddler who was shouting back at them in distress. I could feel the emotions the child was enduring and the dark energy they were putting out to each other and to the other guests who had to endure the noise at two o' clock in the morning. More interestingly, while the guests complained to the hotel staff about the infestation of wasps which swarmed around them, they continued to throw empty ice-cream pots and cups of sugary drinks onto the ground beside them instead of discarding them into nearby bins.

The energy between us could be improved by teaching our next generations about respect for each other and how to work towards fairness and equality. Our way of being seems to be based on comparing ourselves with others and being in constant competition to maintain our personal mode of living, sometimes at the expense of others. We live in an unfair world, so our whole way of being would have to change before there would be a great shift in the dark energy which is constantly rising among us. A world of people having the same dwellings, equal pay and the same provisions sounds far-fetched, but I wonder if this would reduce depression and crime. Some people receive poor wages for working extremely hard and others get huge wads of money for hardly working at all so it's no wonder there is fierce competition for certain occupations and unrest among the population. The dark thoughts people send out about the injustices in their lives turn into dark molecular energy which is absorbed by everyone.

The mechanics of the magnetic rebounding of thought molecules may be similar to the magnetic relationship which the Earth, Moon and other planets in the Universe have with each other. This could mean the molecular substance including energy vibrations, which we give out, has the potential to reach past Earth to other planets then rebound back to us tenfold. I am sure the full effect of the molecular substance and energy vibrations from Earth on other planets is yet to be discovered.

Some people believe there are beings on other solar systems who exist and visit our planet, because they are concerned about the low third-dimensional energy we give out towards them. I have heard of stories about people recalling living on other planets while under hypnosis, but I am not aware of any real proof of there being life beyond our world. It is certainly known that we depend on other planets for our existence. There would be no life on earth if there was no sun and moon, because the sun provides warmth and both the sun and moon cause a magnetic force on the substances and inhabitants of Earth. This magnetic pull causes changes within Earth such as the tides on the sea.

Some midwives joke about expecting to be busy at work when there is a full moon, because it is believed that the higher concentration of the magnetic pull can cause a pregnant woman's amniotic fluid sac around their baby to burst. Water with gravity is thought to be a factor in the push-and-pull transferences of substances. This means we may be reliant and affected by everything on Earth and beyond our solar system.

Scientists were surprised to find that the moon had a magnetic quality, because it was thought to consist of a cool substance. They believed there must be transference of heat or a form of convection for there to be a magnetic substance in existence. I know very little about gravity, chemistry or the effect of molecules on other substances. However, putting all these facts together makes me believe there is much to learn about the attracting, repelling, changing, mixing and merging of molecular substances, especially regarding our energy vibrations.

The high level of water in our bodies might be why magnetic substances and heat are affective in healing us. It may also be why we are drawn to the magnetic healing qualities of water and the sea. The high composition of water within our bodies may be part of the reason why our energy vibrations can be altered and thought transference possible.

Many experiments have been done on icicles, plants and crystals which demonstrate the changes that can occur by exposing them to various music vibrations. Some experts have already extended this research to examine the human energy vibrations when it is exposed to various external vibrations. China categorised internal and external electromagnetic energy as being Chi, which is composed of five elements – wood, fire, earth, metal and water, each containing their own level of vibration and mode of interaction with each other.

Some people have categorised the problems around us as being directly linked to the thought vibrations we absorb and give out. A drained car battery could be a reflection of our own depleted energy, and a sore back may be inadvertently due to carrying too much stress or responsibilities in our lives. It is suggested that we should look within us and change our thought patterns and actions in order to improve our health and that which is around us.

A few countries have embraced what we do know of energy vibrations and are active in working with this energy in a positive manner to improve their Nations' health and their environments. Great Britain is not such a country. Only a selected few are living with the benefits of working with it and the country as a whole suffers. I used to think working with healing energy was for 'Hippies' or people who are crazy in the mind. On the contrary, it is about realising who and what we really are, living as a whole person with two parts of a whole, the physical that we see and the electromagnetic part which we don't. Changing the angle in which we view ourselves can make us look or feel as if we are walking along the 'cliff of reason', but this is due to our conditioning. We can choose to use only one leg and hop clumsily through our life or stride with both our legs without falling over or bumping into our surroundings. In conclusion, we have three eyes, two external and one internal, but only a minority of us chose to use all three. People who are said to be psychic are not gifted, because they have been born with something we don't have. They are gifted because they are born using what we all have.

Living with the Pain

Grief has been a necessary and solitary, selfish emotion I have had to experience. It cut me off from everything and everyone around me. The pain I suffered prompted me to seek a hypnotherapy session. This helped me to remember my past life where I detached myself in a similar sense. The detachment reminded me that when we cut ourselves off from other people we are denying ourselves the love-link energy which helps us thrive. I have felt removed from friends and family but realise those people have shown me great love and understanding, more than they probably realise. This experience has helped me experience the contrast in the high vibrations of the love-link and healing energy against the darkest and lowest of vibrations. I feel love and admiration for myself as it has taken much living and learning to accomplish this lesson. I am only sad that I had to lose my daughter from my life before I could see the woods for the trees. I take comfort in knowing there is a purpose for all that I am and all I am yet to be. In loving myself, I can love those nearest me more.

When we are consumed by pain it is difficult for us to think about anyone else but ourselves. I had to think about my son Cameron, who was only four years old and not yet at primary school when he had to deal with the harsh reality of losing his sister. He is only just finding out about the world around him. I wondered how I could make the loss of his sister make sense to him when it didn't make sense to me. When I read books on how to help a child cope with grief I learned that children are exposed to the idea of death through sources such as the media, watching cartoons and by reading books and comics. Even so, I guess we cannot be completely prepared for death in a general sense from childhood and throughout our lives as the lack of proof of where we come from and go to make us all think differently about it. Our differences in opinions and experiences make it impossible for schools and other establishments teach children in a general sense about death and the afterlife.

While using advice from the books, I told Cameron Natalie's body did not work anymore as she was very, very, very ill with an illness called Cancer. I then added that she could not use her body any longer so came out of her body and is with us without her body as an Angel, watching over us, looking after us. Staff at the nursery school where he attended worked very hard to help him, and his school where he now attends is still helping him with a programme called 'Seasons for Growth.'

The book called 'Badger's Parting Gifts' by Susan Varley explained death to Cameron in a sensitive and logical manner. The most effective books which discuss the subject of death to children are age-specific, so most health visitors or staff at schools can recommend appropriate books.

Cameron has helped me find the light in my life again. He is my rainbow child; the love and laughter he showers me with is a daily tonic. His childlike viewpoint in life is so full of love and fun, untouched by the negativity of adulthood. I make myself take him to play parks and soft-play areas to bask in his happiness. I laugh and smile when he drags me around to play with him and as I watch him having fun with other children. I have to accept the circle of life goes on after our loved ones have gone.

Kevin and Colin have their separate lives, but they, too, have had to overcome the pain of losing their sister. Kevin and his partner had to work through the grief of losing their baby girl, my first and only grandchild. I stood over little Lily's white coffin with Kevin and his partner, unable to shield them from the pain of saying goodbye to their daughter, soon after saying hello. I wondered what was worse – to lose a child or watch your child lose their child. One thing is for sure: the pain of losing a son or daughter, no matter what age, can only be understood when it is experienced first-hand. They have had to move on with their lives just as the rest of Natalie's family have got on with their lives.

Diane, the gifted medium, told me Natalie is happy in the afterlife, helping little babies who have not made it in this world and have passed over. Natalie advised me to continue to help babies into this world. This reading made sense as Natalie studied childcare at college on a dayrelease course arranged by her High School for two years and planned to be a children's nurse before she became sick.

She loved children and animals, especially her white hamster called Domino. It upset her to watch him trying to escape from his cage and running pen. I explained Domino had limited knowledge about his situation as he was unable to see the bigger picture about the threat to his safety like we can. I continued by saying that our life is like that. We can have twists and turns in our path which seem confusing, unfair or pointless, but beings from the spirit world can help us with their higher knowledge if we open our minds to let them. I realise that sometimes we have an awareness of certain things but just need to change the angle from which we look at them to make us think about the impossible being possible.

A wise person said all life's questions can be answered by looking at nature. A great deal of scientific inventions and discoveries have been made by researching the ways of wildlife and nature. I have walked many times surrounded by nature but still find it hard to understand why I am to be without my daughter. Natalie explained we worked together as a team in our past lives and are still a team between our two worlds. Writing this book together could possibly be part of the larger plan.

I did not have much interest in or knowledge about Spirit and the afterlife until my world came crashing down when I suffered loss through my divorce. This traumatic experience prompted me to search for the spiritual part of me I always felt was missing. Even though I was not fully aware of Spirit existing through the earlier part of my life, I now understand they have always been there and intervened at crucial times. Some people are ready to hear what people like me have learned about our energy system and the afterlife, but many are not. I hope I have enlightened some souls to at least think about it.

I have to live without my daughter physically in my life but understand now more than ever that love is eternal. It is a chemical substance, an emotion which can cross all barriers of time and space. Most people strive to bask in the emotion of love, to be loved, to fit in and be accepted by the people around them. I believe this is the basis of why we behave the way we do. We are naturally happy, carefree, loving and whole and connected beings, but our high vibrations are continually tested and disfigured by our limited 'Earth plane thinking' and extreme experiences of life.

I was unable to look through my daughter's things for keepsakes but I was given the Hunter Wellington boots she bought to protect herself from the elements. This was the footwear she bought which was practical rather than fashionable, but it was in vain. I find it difficult to look at them because they were supposed to protect her just like I was supposed to protect her, but couldn't.

The time I have spent with my daughter seems so short but precious. I am glad we took time to have a tight lingering hug before bedtime one night as I can still feel the love and sensations of that mother-daughter hug today. When we embraced, I asked Natalie to close her eyes and feel all the sensations of our love in the hug so she could remember them and reach me when she was gone. I think this exercise may have benefited me more than her, because when we are in Spirit we can see, feel and hear the living but the living can find it hard to sense Spirit.

There is no doubt that grief is exceptionally painful. Many people who are grieving feel time does not heal. I concluded that I could either stay stuck in my pain or try to reach happiness by riding through the waves of my loss and find my purpose in life. I found my thoughts and reactions had a great impact on my experience of events and how I overcome them. Life is as much an illusion as the ground we walk on. The thin layer of tarmac on our roads and pavements is only a tiny fraction of the earth it covers so why do we generally choose to see the thin illusion rather than widen our view to see the whole?

The hurt from loss made me wear tinted glasses and recoil from people and life to protect myself from more pain. I disconnected myself further as I believed I was different due to being more interested in the spiritual side of my life than the hum-drum basics of human life. However, I realise that I am not so different and perhaps needed to be jolted back into living in this world.

I understand we have to come to our own conclusions when trying to accept the loss of our loved ones. I found my resolve in the knowledge that there is an afterlife where my daughter lives on, albeit in another way. Some may believe I merely want there to be an afterlife so I can continue to keep Natalie alive. My experience of working with healing energy and contact with Spirit before and after her death has shown me that my views are not just the wishful thinking of a grieving mother.

Part of the mourning process at death involves the withdrawal of the deceased's energy from those he or she may have shared their life with. The closer and more intimate the relationship, the longer this untangling can take. It is possible people choose their mode of exit from this world according to how they believe their family and friends may cope with their departure and the detangling of energy. This knowledge helps me come to terms with Natalie having to go through what she did before she died. Perhaps, she was giving us all time to slowly untangle and loosen the attachments for us to cope better and let her go, but I didn't let go. I was flying high, speeding around with her, holding on for dear life. In time, I will have to come to terms with living here on Earth without her and stop trying to hem her spirit in beside me. I take comfort in knowing that she comes to visit us all and chats with me regularly.

Through a gifted medium called Liz at the Stirling Spiritualist Church, Natalie said my teaching about Spirit and the spirit world made her calm and at peace when she passed. She was surprised how easy it was when she did leave as all she did was close her eyes then opened them to find she was a spirit in the spirit world. She did not pass alone; all her loved ones were there to welcome her.

She spent time in the Church library while waiting to make contact with me. Liz said Natalie pointed to an area on one of the book shelves, saying: "Mum's book will go nicely right there." I felt reassured Natalie was happy with the book and pleased she was aware of my plan to donate one to the Church.

I thought I had the purpose for my daughter leaving this world wrapped up and put into a conclusion bag, but she changed my thinking. She said she saw the full picture of why she had to leave when she did but I would not understand everything until I joined her in the spirit world. She said she would have liked to stay longer, but it was not to be. She had no regrets about how she lived her short life as she lived it to the full.

She told me to slow down because there are not more than twenty-four hours in a day. I laughed when she followed this advice by saying that she never stops over there as it's all so exciting. She loves being in the spirit world, visiting all the places we talked about during our cosy nights in, especially the Great Halls of Learning. She talked about how I prayed for her to be happy without pain. I was to be happy as my prayers were answered. She knew how proud I am of her, but now the roles were reversed as she was proud of her mum. At the end of her visit, I give her a virtual cuddle and let her go to continue living a better life in a better world until her next visit.

Natalie asked me to put some words in one of the hymn books in the Spiritualist Church to help link her with the members and visitors of the Church. I thought about the deep love I have felt for her since her birth. This inspired me to write a verse which sums up my life as a midwife watching old souls coming back for new lives and the profound emotions most mothers experience when they meet their baby for the first time at birth.

Timeless Stars

We're on a journey, working hard to do right.
Always moving onwards while guided by the light
My passion, your glory. Our love, our story.
I see them in tiny eyes – our timeless, twinkling stars.

Hearts beat faster as they find their way.
Great expectations for a brand-new day.
My passion, your glory. Our love, our story.
I see them in tiny eyes – our timeless, twinkling stars.

I smile as you embrace with profound emotion.
Two hearts immersed in a spiritual love potion.
My passion, your glory. Our love, our story.
I see them in tiny eyes – our timeless, twinkling stars.

Loving and learning, 'as above as below'.
New beginnings, no endings to reap what we sow.
My passion, your glory. Our love, our story.
I see them in tiny eyes. Shine on our timeless stars.

Keeping the love-link cords strong between all that lives and maintaining balance in our world could be the key to our ever-lasting existence. However, the energy of the population, Earth and our solar system may be becoming out of balance. Perhaps, this is why people like me are risking being ridiculed as we step forward to share our experiences. Bridges can be mended, but not always. People experience events and interactions from different angles so cords cannot always be re-connected. In these circumstances, unconditional forgiveness may go a long way to dispel the darkness even when disconnection persists.

The characters and events in my life story no longer exist as we have all changed and moved on. I spent many hours thinking about how I can help save our world but I failed to realise I had to first change and save myself. I cannot change my past, but I can use what I have learnt and refuse to let it affect my future. With this in mind, I chose to forgive all my wrong-doing and all those who have done me wrong so I can move on and enjoy the next chapter of my life.

I have stopped making excuses and apologising for who and what I am. I no longer try to fit in with other people's idea or understanding of life as I know my experiences with Spirit and healing energy are real. I now enjoy attending clubs and workshops to learn and have fun with like-minded people. My hair has grown back as if I had never lost it. I have joined a weight-loss programme to try and find the girl within me again. I spend quality time with my family and friends while focusing on rebuilding my life, accepting what is and will be.

Just as I was writing these last words, the rock band Runrig came to my town to perform their last two live performances. I opened the box containing Natalie's Wellington boots and put them on my feet. I carried her in my heart as I walked in her boots to a gig I knew she would manage to attend. I snapped a photo of a rainbow which shone over the gig and the astounding view of Stirling Castle. I looked up into the sky and thought: *'Where are you?'* I heard Natalie shout back: "I'm here!" The audience around me clapped and cheered while a fitting beat had me dancing the sword dance in my daughter's boots.

A lovely woman beside me told me she found it difficult to be at the gig without her husband since he had died. She continued: "He used to stand behind me to make sure people didn't bump into me or push past me." I replied: "He must be here because I haven't seen anyone push past you." I glanced behind the woman at the vacant space and suddenly thought: we are all dancing under the same sky with our loved ones, regardless of whether it is their feet or heart which dances with us.

My friend was in her back garden a mile from the gig, listening to thousands of people singing 'Loch Lomond', a song which has been adopted as Scotland's national anthem. She heard everyone singing in unison, linking together as they shone out great love for the song, the band, for everyone and everything in Scotland. I am glad I put the sadness of losing Natalie to one side and pulled on her boots to enjoy this powerful uplifting experience.

As I continue without my daughter physically in my life, I have to dust myself down and keep my chin up when I watch mothers and daughters out having fun together. I smile when I watch women hug their new-born babies as I know the deep love they will share until it is time for either one to move on to the spirit world.

I try to accept the special times I looked forward to with my daughter will never happen. There are so many things I wish I had done with Natalie, but all I can do now is carry my love for her in my heart and treasure all the memories which are to last me my lifetime.

When I was young, I thought I was invincible and everyone lived forever. It has taken much living to realise we are all on an unpredictable timer until we return home. With this in mind, before I walk away from the experience of losing my daughter, I would like to say: “Take the time to make many happy memories. Don’t put off today what you could have done yesterday as for some, no matter what age you are, there may not be a tomorrow.” If Natalie was able to join me in bringing this part of our journey to a close, I guess she would say: “Feel the love within and around you.” Most of all: “Keep it happy!”

So, there I was, sitting on my sofa with the sun shining through the window. I tucked my pen away and looked at the photo of my daughter next to me. I smiled as I felt immense love, not heartache. A huge weight lifted from my shoulders, my work was done. Replacing the foot-rest, I stood up and ventured out-doors to look at the world with different eyes. I listened to music as I walked with Harvey in my toe-capped shoes. The wind brushed against the energy pulsating in my hands. My gaze shifted from the little white feathers on the ground to the spring flowers and shrubbery along the country walk-way. As I raised my head higher to acknowledge the people around me, geese flew overhead. They called out, rejoicing – the winter was nearly over. The colder and darker days were coming to an end, at least for a while.

ACKNOWLEDGEMENTS

I would like to thank my family, friends and work colleagues for all their support. A special 'thank you' goes to Annette Munnich, Diane White, Lino G Rocha, Patsy, Paul Williamson and Sam Wall. A huge 'thank you' goes to the members of the Stirling Spiritualist Church – especially to Liz Buchan, who helped me find my Spirit, my true self. Thank you, Monika of Ochil Writers' Group and Daphne of Alloa Writers for helping me find my words. Thank you to the Resonate Arts House Singers who helped my soul to sing. Thank you to all those in spirit, especially Natalie and my dad for their help and wise teaching. I regard publication of this book as a team effort as I have received much advice from many kind people, so I thank you all. Finally, thank you to all those who have been entwined with my life experiences and have allowed me to share those moments. I look forward to those who have yet to come forward and play a part in my last chapter on Earth.

BIBLIOGRAPHY

Shine, Betty – 'Mind to Mind', Transworld Digital, 2011, ISBN 1448125154

Williamson, Paul – 'Earth Warriors', Animal Dreaming Publishing, 2017

Jackson, Laura Lyn – 'The Light Between Us', Cornerstone Digital, 2015, ISBN 0812987926

Donne, Kate – 'The Wit and Wisdom of Bobby 'Chicken Legs' Muldoon trilogy, Book 1, Publish Nation , 2016

Lavato, Anita and Dr.Wilkins, James – 'A Baby's Viewpoint of Life and Death', Life Sentence, 2013, ISBN 1622451171

Varley, Susan – 'Badger's Parting Gifts', Anderson Press, 2013, ISBN-13 978-1849395144

ABOUT THE AUTHOR

Helen Nicol was born and raised in Stirling, Scotland. She married her first husband in 1985 at the age of eighteen-years-old. She moved to Germany and lived as an Army wife for nearly seven years before she returned home to Scotland. She was a single parent with two sons and one daughter for fourteen years until she moved to the Scottish Highlands and married her second husband. She had another son in 2011 and move back to her hometown in 2015 to be with her daughter when her daughter was very poorly.

During Helen's life she has been a Secretary, Computer Keeyer, Shop Keeper, Actress, Singer, Dancer, Healer, Holistic Therapist, Researcher, Midwife and Author.

She wrote the poem 'Heavenly Message' which was adapted by Lino G Rocha to produce the song 'Heavenly Message'. The poem and song were the inspiration for the book 'Heavenly Message: My Journey to Natalie's Song'.

She appeared on The UK Lottery Stars television programme 2015 with Anton du Beke to create a bigger awareness of the good work of Strathcarron Hospice at Home. She has been active in raising funds for Cancer related charities with her family and friends. As a Team, over £12,000 has been raised off and online.

Helen lives with her husband and son in the Central belt of Scotland. She still works as a midwife, Healer and Holistic Therapist and is busy producing her second book 'My Little Friend Batbird' which was inspired by the creation of 'Heavenly Message: My Journey to Natalie's Song'.

The link to our charity work
https://www.justgiving.com/teams/nataliegray
Helen's Blog on Wordpress
http://heavenlymessage.co.uk/
Email: heavenlymessagepublishing@yahoo.com